API Management with Bruno

Postman's Super-Alternative to Build, Test and Deploy APIs in Multi-Cloud Environment

Lyria Tharax

Published by: GitforGits

Publisher: Sonal Dhandre

www.gitforgits.com

support@gitforgits.com

Printed in India

First Printing: January 2025

ISBN: 978-81-984316-3-9

Cover Design by: Kitten Publishing

Prologue

Postman once reigned supreme in the world of API development. Its user-friendly interface and extensive feature set made it a popular tool among developers worldwide. For many, it provided a familiar environment for developing, testing, and managing APIs. However, as our projects became more complex and the need for efficiency grew, I found myself wanting for a tool that provided a lighter, more agile approach. Because of this need, I looked into Bruno, a new option that rethinks API management. Bruno eliminated unnecessary complexity, resulting in an experience centered on speed, simplicity, and powerful command-line integration. This book grew out of my own experience transitioning from traditional API development tools to an environment that encourages creativity and efficiency.

With this updated edition, I hope you'll come along for a ride that will change the way you think about API management and design forever. By interacting with the scenarios presented here, you will be able to better understand the difficulties we encounter on a daily basis. I wrote this book to demonstrate how to use Bruno's capabilities to design, build, test, deploy, and manage every stage of the API lifecycle. You'll see how simple commands and well-thought-out scripts can replace repetitive manual tasks, freeing you up to focus on what really matters: problem solving and value creation. I'll walk you through creating a modern development environment, writing clear and maintainable API blueprints, and embedding business logic to bring your endpoints to life. You will also learn how to secure your API using token-based authentication and granular authorization. The book continues with automated testing, debugging, and integration with third-party services, which ensures that your APIs are not only functional but also resilient and scalable.

This edition features practical, step-by-step exercises that I personally tested in my development environment. It provides a distinct combination of hands-on examples, live debugging sessions, and custom automation scripts that turn abstract concepts into practical skills. Throughout this book, I'll be sharing my own experiences, challenges, and insights to help you make the transition from familiar tools like Postman and Insomnia to the dynamic, efficient world of Bruno.

Content

Preface

If you're an API practitioner, this book will show you how to use Bruno to its maximum capacity for managing your API lifecycle. Bruno is a new alternative to Postman and Insomnia; this practical book will teach you how to use it for API design, development, testing, deployment, and oversight. The book is less concerned with helping you become an API Management expert than it is with showing you how to make the most of Bruno's features so that you can efficiently complete tasks in the real world.

The chapters cover topics such as creating a safe and scalable development environment, using the Bruno command line interface (CLI), and creating API blueprints with Bru Lang that are easy to understand and maintain. You'll learn how to embed business logic, manage data transformations, and implement robust error handling to build dynamic endpoints that respond to real-time events. In an effort to protect sensitive information, practical implementations of OAuth 2.0 authorization, JWT authentication, and effective secret management are implemented. Your API's reliability and scalability under different conditions can be further assured with automated testing and live debugging sessions.

You can automate mundane tasks and expand your API's functionality with the help of the advanced integrations covered in this book. These integrations allow you to connect to popular platforms like AWS, Jira, GitHub, and Jenkins. Additionally, you will become an expert at configuring and executing webhooks and event-driven actions, which are crucial for keeping your API in sync with external systems. As a result of the practical examples and scripts provided in each chapter, this book is a must-have for anyone working on APIs in the modern day.

In this book you will learn to:

- Use Bruno CLI via npm for simplified installation and guarantees an up-to-date API management toolkit.
- Create clear API blueprints for designing and building robust endpoints.
- Integrate JWT authentication for secure API access while supporting scalable, stateless user management practices.
- Integrate OAuth 2.0 for fine-grained authorization, and to control access to sensitive API resources.
- Implement secrets management via environment variables to protect credentials and maintains secure configuration.
- Implement automated test suites to validate API functionality across all endpoints.
- Carry out real-time debugging and logging of API interactions during live operations.

- Write custom automation scripts to streamline testing, deployment, and data management across API workflows.
- Integrate with third-party services like Jira, GitHub, Jenkins, and AWS.
- Work around webhooks and event-driven actions to respond real-time events.

GitforGits

Prerequisites

This book is intended to empower Postman Users and all API practitioners to fully utilize Bruno's capabilities in managing all aspects of the API lifecycle. All you need to know is basic understanding of API and its lifecycle to begin with this book.

Codes Usage

Are you in need of some helpful code examples to assist you in your programming and documentation? Look no further! Our book offers a wealth of supplemental material, including code examples and exercises.

Not only is this book here to aid you in getting your job done, but you have our permission to use the example code in your programs and documentation. However, please note that if you are reproducing a significant portion of the code, we do require you to contact us for permission.

But don't worry, using several chunks of code from this book in your program or answering a question by citing our book and quoting example code does not require permission. But if you do choose to give credit, an attribution typically includes the title, author, publisher, and ISBN. For example, " API Management with Bruno by Lyria Tharax".

If you are unsure whether your intended use of the code examples falls under fair use or the permissions outlined above, please do not hesitate to reach out to us at support@gitforgits.com.

We are happy to assist and clarify any concerns.

Acknowledgement

I owe a tremendous debt of gratitude to GitforGits, for their unflagging enthusiasm and wise counsel throughout the entire process of writing this book. Their knowledge and careful editing helped make sure the piece was useful for people of all reading levels and comprehension skills. In addition, I'd like to thank everyone involved in the publishing process for their efforts in making this book a reality. Their efforts, from copyediting to advertising, made the project what it is today.

Finally, I'd like to express my gratitude to everyone who has shown me unconditional love and encouragement throughout my life. Their support was crucial to the completion of this book. I appreciate your help with this endeavour and your continued interest in my career.

Chapter 1: Getting Started with Bruno

Overview

Bruno enters the stage at a time when established tools like Postman have earned a strong reputation among API practitioners. Postman built its position on a robust ecosystem that empowered developers to create, test, and manage APIs efficiently. Its feature set and integration capabilities made it a default choice for many who sought a dependable solution to support their API workflows. Over the years, developers have relied on Postman for a wide range of tasks, from constructing detailed API calls to automating testing routines, which enhanced productivity and contributed significantly to smoother development cycles. However, even with its solid reputation and widespread adoption, the evolution of API development practices and scaling requirements has presented new challenges that necessitate alternatives. The growth of cloud-based systems and microservices architectures has pushed developers to reconsider the balance between functionality and resource efficiency, ssthereby creating openings for newer, more streamlined tools to compete effectively in the modern API ecosystem.

Postman began as a freemium platform that provided extensive capabilities at no cost for many of its basic features, enabling developers to explore and execute API-related tasks without financial commitment. As the tool expanded its functionalities, its freemium model naturally transitioned to a structure where advanced features and higher usage limits required paid subscriptions. Over time, this shift resulted in higher expenses for organizations that depended on the tool for everyday operations. As teams scaled up and projects grew in complexity, the costs associated with accessing premium features started to become a significant consideration. Additionally, Postman's interface, while rich with features, began to feel increasingly bloated, especially for those who preferred lightweight, nimble tools that offer speed and simplicity without compromising essential functionalities. The rising operational costs, combined with the growing demand for leaner and more agile API development tools, paved the way for Bruno to emerge as an appealing alternative.

Developers have long appreciated a tool that not only supports a wide array of functionalities but also maintains efficiency and ease of use. Postman's evolution into a more resource-intensive solution has driven some teams to search for alternatives that can match their technical requirements without incurring excessive overheads. Bruno steps into this space with an emphasis on simplicity, speed, and an uncluttered user experience that resonates with the modern API developer. With Bruno, the objective is to offer a tool that preserves essential API development capabilities while streamlining the workflow. Its design intentionally minimizes unnecessary complexity and heavy resource usage, thereby allowing developers to concentrate on delivering functional, well-structured APIs without the distractions of extraneous features. This shift in focus aligns with the needs of teams that are adept at handling API challenges and are ready to adopt a tool that is more agile and cost-effective in comparison to a platform that has evolved into a more expensive and bulkier solution.

Embracing Bruno means adopting a new mindset in API development—one that values efficient operations and the ability to quickly transition from designing endpoints to deploying fully operational APIs. The tool is built with a practical approach, which ensures that every command and feature is designed to facilitate the rapid execution of tasks without unnecessary overhead. Developers familiar with Postman's extensive offerings may find Bruno refreshing due to its lean interface and focus on core functionalities. By streamlining routine tasks and automating several aspects of the API lifecycle, Bruno empowers users to concentrate on delivering high-quality APIs that align with real-world operational demands. This emphasis on practical utility, combined with an intuitive command structure, allows teams to maintain productivity and achieve faster turnaround times. Ultimately, Bruno positions itself as a valuable alternative for those who seek a robust yet unobtrusive tool to complement their API development processes.

The emergence of Bruno is also indicative of a broader trend in software development where efficiency and simplicity take precedence over feature-heavy platforms. Modern development teams increasingly prioritize tools that integrate seamlessly into continuous integration and continuous deployment pipelines, facilitate real-time debugging, and offer flexible customization options. Bruno is engineered to address these needs by providing a lightweight, yet powerful solution that bridges the gap between the need for advanced API functionalities and the desire for a lean, cost-effective tool. Its approach involves a clear separation of concerns, where each feature is designed to perform a specific role in the API lifecycle. This allows developers to adopt a modular approach to building and managing APIs, where they can quickly implement, test, and optimize their solutions in a coherent workflow. The result is a tool that is not only easier to use but also aligns closely with modern agile development practices, making it an attractive option for experienced professionals who demand both performance and simplicity.

As developers consider the transition from established tools like Postman to alternatives such as Bruno, they must evaluate the trade-offs between familiarity and innovation. While Postman offers a well-tested ecosystem, its increasing complexity and cost can impede agility, particularly in fast-paced environments where lean operational models are key. Bruno addresses these concerns by offering a streamlined experience that eliminates unnecessary bloat and focuses on the essentials of API development. It provides developers with a platform that is both accessible and potent, enabling a smooth transition for those looking to optimize their workflows. The learning curve is designed to be manageable for professionals who are already well-versed in API fundamentals, ensuring that the migration from traditional tools is not only feasible but also rewarding. By focusing on delivering a balanced mix of functionality and ease of use, Bruno represents a strategic choice for teams that prioritize speed, cost-efficiency, and operational simplicity in their API development endeavors.

The whole transition to a tool like Bruno is as much about embracing change as it is about enhancing technical workflows. For developers who have relied on Postman for years, the decision to explore Bruno might be driven by the need to overcome the challenges of escalating costs and an overloaded interface. Bruno's design philosophy is rooted in the belief that a tool should empower its users without overwhelming them with extraneous features. This philosophy is evident in every aspect of its design—from the minimalistic command structure to the robust automation capabilities that reduce manual overhead. As API development continues to evolve, tools that offer a leaner, more focused approach will increasingly find favor among those who appreciate efficiency and practicality. The introduction of Bruno, with its streamlined functionality and clear focus on the core aspects of API development, presents an opportunity to reimagine how developers approach the API lifecycle. This new perspective encourages a shift away from heavy, resource-intensive solutions toward more agile and cost-effective alternatives that align with the dynamic needs of modern software projects.

The Postman's evolution into a more expensive and bulky solution is not intended to diminish its value or legacy in the API development community. Instead, it highlights the natural progression of software tools as they adapt to changing technological landscapes and user requirements. Developers have long recognized the merits of Postman, and its influence remains significant in shaping best practices for API development. However, as development needs evolve, so too must the tools that support them. Bruno emerges as a viable option that not only meets the current demands for efficiency and simplicity but also anticipates future challenges by offering a flexible, user-friendly platform. Its streamlined approach to API design, development, testing, security, and automation promises to make the entire lifecycle more manageable, particularly for experienced professionals who seek to optimize their workflows. This chapter sets the stage for a deeper exploration of Bruno's features, ensuring that users are equipped with the knowledge and practical insights needed to harness its full potential in their API development endeavors.

In this chapter, we will begin with discovering the features that make Bruno an ideal platform for designing, developing, and managing APIs. We then learn through the installation of the Bruno CLI and the configuration of Bru Lang within our Linux environment, ensuring that our setup is ready for advanced development tasks. Next, we will take a tour of Bruno's interface and command structure, which will familiarize us with the navigation, built-in commands, and interactive features that make working with Bruno efficient and intuitive. As we progress, we will gain hands-on experience with commands that initialize projects, execute scripts, and manage configurations, paving the way for practical API development. This chapter will set the stage for a smooth transition into building and managing APIs, providing us with the foundational knowledge and skills needed to take full advantage of Bruno's capabilities.

Bruno's Capabilities for API Lifecycle

So, Bruno's got all these features that help with every step of API development, like the design process and ongoing management. Right now, we're going to take a look at how Bruno sets up a neat, efficient, and interactive environment for creating, testing, and tweaking APIs. With its super cool features, we can make the whole API lifecycle a breeze, making sure our projects are built with clarity, agility, and strength.

Design First Approach

Intuitive Blueprint Creation

Bruno introduces a design-first approach that lets us quickly create detailed API blueprints. We define endpoints, specify request and response structures, and construct data schemas using a declarative syntax. This intuitive approach minimizes overhead and enables us to capture the overall structure of our API projects accurately.

Validation and Consistency Checks

Next feature that I like the most is its integrated validation system. As we design our API blueprints, Bruno continuously checks for consistency and adherence to the specified schema. This real-time validation minimizes errors early in the development process and maintains the integrity of the design. This feature is particularly valuable when dealing with complex request and response models, as it ensures that every element conforms to a consistent set of standards.

Clear Command Structure for Design

The command structure in Bruno is purposefully streamlined to make design tasks straightforward. Every command and configuration setting is designed to be self-explanatory, reducing the learning curve and promoting rapid adoption. We can quickly map out our API's endpoints and data flows, confident in the fact that Bruno's organized framework will help us avoid common pitfalls associated with poorly structured designs. This clarity is essential when collaborating in teams, as it provides a common language and format that everyone can follow.

Flexible, Lightweight and Easy Integration

Lightweight and Powerful Development Environment

Once the design is in place, Bruno transitions seamlessly into the development phase. The tool offers a lightweight environment that emphasizes efficiency without sacrificing functionality. We benefit from a coding interface that supports the entire API development process—from writing code for endpoints to embedding business logic into our application. This environment is optimized to keep distractions to a minimum while maximizing our ability to implement robust API functionalities.

Bru Lang for Expressive Coding

Now here, at the heart of Bruno's development capabilities lies Bru language that simplifies coding for APIs. Bru Lang is designed to be both expressive and concise, allowing us to write code that is easy to understand and maintain. It helps to rapidly implement core endpoints and integrate complex business logic with minimal boilerplate. The language's syntax is engineered to reflect the underlying design principles of Bruno.

Seamless Integration of Business Logic

The embedding of business logic into API endpoints helps in transforming design into a functional service. Bruno facilitates this by providing a suite of tools that integrate coding and configuration seamlessly. We can define conditional operations, manage data transformations, and handle error conditions directly within our API code. This integration reduces the need for external tools and ensures that every aspect of our API—whether it's a simple data retrieval or a complex transactional operation—is handled within a unified framework.

Error Handling and Data Transformation

Robust API development requires mechanisms for managing data transformations and handling errors gracefully. Bruno offers a set of features dedicated to these tasks. We can define custom error handlers and data transformers that ensure our API behaves predictably under a range of conditions. This built-in functionality means that we are less reliant on third-party libraries or additional code, thereby the troubleshooting becomes far easy, as the system provides clear insights into where issues may arise during development.

Real-time, Scalable and Robust Management

Streamlined API Lifecycle Management

Bruno's capabilities extend far beyond the initial development phase. Once our API is built, Bruno provides powerful tools for managing the entire lifecycle of the service. We can monitor performance, apply updates, and manage deployments from within a single cohesive platform.

Integrated Automation and CI/CD Support

A key aspect of modern API management is the ability to automate routine tasks and integrate them into continuous integration/continuous deployment (CI/CD) pipelines. Bruno supports automation through its command-line interface (CLI) and scripting capabilities within Bru Lang. We can automate test runs, deploy updates, and even roll back changes if necessary.

Real-Time Debugging and Monitoring

Maintaining a live API in production comes with its own set of challenges. Bruno addresses these challenges by offering real-time debugging and monitoring features. We can trace API requests and responses as they occur, leveraging detailed logs and live analytics to diagnose issues immediately. This capability aids in identifying and resolving errors, and also helps in optimizing performance over time.

Scalable and Flexible Management

Most important is that Bruno is built with scalability in mind. The management interface is flexible enough to accommodate the evolving needs of our API, whether we are introducing new endpoints, integrating additional services, or scaling up for higher traffic. This flexibility ensures that Bruno remains a reliable partner throughout the lifecycle of our API, adapting to changes without requiring extensive rework or the adoption of new tools.

End-to-End API Lifecycle Fulfillment

A Unified Workflow from Design to Deployment

From the moment we start designing an API blueprint to the point where we are managing live deployments, Bruno provides a consistent and integrated experience. This holistic approach means that every step—be it designing, coding, testing, or managing—is interconnected to maintain a smooth workflow without needing to switch between disparate tools or environments.

Efficiency Through Integrated Tooling

Every feature, whether it's an automation script or a debugging function, is designed to work seamlessly with the rest of the platform. This integration is particularly beneficial for teams that aim to reduce overhead and focus on high-value development tasks. We can quickly iterate on designs, implement changes, and see the results in real time, all within the same environment. This efficiency translates to faster development cycles and more robust APIs, as every aspect of the process is streamlined for optimal performance.

Flexibility and Agility in API Development

The flexibility of Bruno, such as its modular design allows us to adopt the features that best suit our project needs while leaving room for customization and innovation. Whether we are migrating from a more cumbersome tool or starting a new project from scratch, Bruno offers the agility needed to adapt to changing requirements. This adaptability is quite a key in modern software development, where rapid iteration and continuous improvement are the crticial norms to success.

Ultimately, Bruno is not just a tool for managing API projects; it is a practical platform built to address real-world challenges in API development. By supporting the entire lifecycle—from design to deployment—Bruno empowers us to create APIs that are robust, scalable, and ready for production environments. Its interactive features and streamlined workflows ensure that we can focus on solving problems and delivering high-quality services without being bogged down by unnecessary complexity.

In this way, Bruno's capabilities for API lifecycle management cover the full spectrum of development activities. We witness an environment where design, development, and management converge into a single, cohesive system—one that is tailored to meet the challenges of today's fast-paced and ever-evolving API landscape.

Installing Bruno CLI and Configuring Bru Lang

So here, we'll install the Bruno CLI using npm and configure Bru Lang to set up our development environment for the Lumina API project. The use of npm for installation helps to streamline the process, especially for those already familiar with JavaScript package management.

In the below, I have quickly outlined the practical steps to get Bruno CLI up and running on your Linux system:

Bruno CLI via npm

There's an easier way to get the latest version of Bruno CLI, and that's to use npm to install it globally. This way, you always have the latest version right from the npm repository.

Verify Node.js and npm Installation

First open your terminal and run:

```
node -v
npm -v
```

If these commands output version numbers, you're ready to continue. If not, install Node.js and npm from the official website or via your package manager.

Install Bruno CLI Globally

With npm ready, run the following command to install Bruno CLI globally:

```
npm install -g @usebruno/cli
```

This command downloads and installs Bruno CLI on your system, making the `bruno` command available from any terminal window. Once installed, verify the installation by running:

```
bruno --version
```

You should see the version number printed, confirming that Bruno CLI is correctly installed.

Configuring Bru Lang

Bru Lang is the domain-specific language used within Bruno to facilitate API development tasks. After installing Bruno CLI, the next step involves setting up Bru Lang by creating a configuration file that informs the CLI about the development environment settings.

First we create a configuration directory:

```
mkdir -p ~/.bruno
```

Inside this directory, we then create a configuration file named **`config.json`** using **`nano`**:

```
nano ~/.bruno/config.json
```

In the configuration file, insert the necessary settings. I have given below a sample configuration for your understanding:

```
{
  "bru_lang": {
    "version": "1.0.0",
    "default_environment": "linux",
    "editor": "vim",
    "log_level": "info"
  },
  "api_defaults": {
    "base_url": "http://localhost:3000",
    "timeout": 5000
  }
}
```

This JSON structure configures the Bru Lang version, sets the default environment to Linux, specifies an editor (e.g., vim), and sets a logging level. It also defines default API settings such as the base URL and request timeout.

After this, save the file and exit the editor by pressing Ctrl+X, then Y, and Enter.

Now if you want to ensure that the configuration is recognized, simply run the following command:

```
bruno config --show
```

This command should display the current configuration settings, confirming that the Bru Lang configuration is active.

Now that you've installed Bruno CLI and set up Bru Lang, it's a good idea to make sure everything's working right. You can do this by running this easy command:

```
bruno bru-lang --version
```

The output should indicate the version of Bru Lang, confirming that it is properly configured alongside Bruno CLI.

Alternatively, you can create a sample Bru Lang script to test the environment. To do this, simply create a file named **`sample.bru`** with the following script:

```
// sample.bru
endpoint /hello {
  method: GET;
  response: {
    status: 200;
    body: "Hello, API world!"
  }
}
```

This script defines a basic API endpoint that responds with a greeting message. Next, execute the script by running:

```
bruno run sample.bru
```

If everything is correctly installed, you should see output indicating that the **`/hello`** endpoint is registered, along with the expected response details.

With this one-time setup, we can focus on designing, building, testing, and managing APIs without having to go back and re-do the installation process.

Bruno's Interface and Command Structure

Once we've installed Bruno CLI and configured Bru Lang on our Linux environment, we'll dive into the interface and command structure that form the backbone of our API development experience. First, we'll take a look at Bruno's command-line navigation, detailing the commands we'll use throughout our project. Then, we'll discover how to use the built-in commands, explore interactive features, and understand the overall syntax that makes Bruno both powerful and intuitive.

Navigating Bruno CLI

Now let us recall that when we launch Bruno in our terminal, we are greeted with a streamlined interface that minimizes clutter and emphasizes efficiency. The interface is designed with clarity in mind, presenting us with a clear prompt and a set of commands organized into logical groups.

By typing:

```
bruno help
```

we gain access to a comprehensive list of available commands. This built-in help command is our first stop for understanding Bruno's capabilities. The output lists commands grouped by functionality—ranging from blueprint design and endpoint configuration to automation and debugging—each accompanied by a brief description. This makes it easy for us to identify which command aligns with our current task.

Let us take a look at some of the most fundamental commands that we will use frequently as below:

- **`bruno init`**: This command initializes a new API project. It creates the necessary file structure and configuration files that set the stage for developing our API.
- **`bruno run <file>`**: With this command, we can execute Bru Lang scripts, enabling us to test endpoints, simulate API responses, or run automation scripts.
- **`bruno config`**: As we previously learned, this command helps us view and update our configuration settings. It is instrumental in ensuring that our development environment remains consistent.
- **`bruno status`**: This provides a real-time snapshot of our current API project, showing active endpoints, active sessions, and any background processes that might be running.
- **`bruno logs`**: For monitoring purposes, this command retrieves logs generated by our API during testing or live operations. It is invaluable when we need to debug issues.

They're our go-to tools for getting around in the project, and they're all designed to be easy to understand. They all follow the same syntax, which shows how Bruno is built to be modular and intuitive.

Exploring Command Syntax

Bruno's command syntax is designed to be straightforward and modular. At its core, every command follows the structure:

```
bruno <command> [sub-command] [options] [arguments]
```

Here,

- **Command**: This is the primary instruction we wish to execute (e.g., **`init`**, **`run`**, **`config`**).
- **Sub-command**: Some commands are further divided into sub-commands that allow for more granular operations (for example, **`config --show`** to display current settings).

- **Options**: Options modify the behavior of commands. They are typically preceded by dashes (e.g., **`--verbose`** for detailed output).
- **Arguments**: These are the values or files that the command operates on (such as the filename when running a Bru Lang script).

For instance, to run a script with detailed logging enabled, we might use:

```
bruno run sample.bru --verbose
```

Built-In Commands

Bruno comes with an extensive suite of built-in commands designed to assist us through every stage of the API lifecycle. A few of these commands include:

bruno init

When we start a new project, this command creates a directory structure tailored for API development. It sets up directories for endpoints, configurations, and tests, along with a basic project configuration file.

```
bruno init my-api-project
```

This command initializes a new project named my-api-project, setting up the groundwork for further development.

bruno run

This command is used to execute Bru Lang scripts that define our API endpoints or automation tasks. It reads the script file and processes it, registering endpoints or performing specified operations.

```
bruno run endpoints.bru
```

Here, we execute a script named endpoints.bru which may define various API endpoints. The output confirms that the endpoints are active and provides real-time feedback on their status.

bruno config

Beyond just viewing our current settings, this command allows us to update configuration parameters dynamically. We can change the default environment, update logging levels, or modify API defaults.

```
bruno config --set log_level=debug
```

This command updates our configuration to set the logging level to debug, ensuring we receive detailed output during subsequent operations.

bruno status

A quick snapshot of our project's current state is accessible via this command. It provides an overview of active services, running processes, and system health.

```
bruno status
```

This command returns a summary that helps us quickly identify if any issues need addressing before proceeding further.

bruno logs

Monitoring and troubleshooting are key components of API development. The logs command aggregates outputs from various operations, allowing us to review historical activity or troubleshoot errors.

```
bruno logs --tail
```

The **`--tail`** option allows us to view the most recent entries, providing a live feed that is especially useful during active development sessions.

Sample Program: Command Structure in Action

We will walk through a practical session that showcases Bruno's interface and command structure in action. This interactive example simulates initializing a new project, running a sample script, and verifying the setup.

Project Initialization

We begin by initializing our project. In the terminal, we execute:

```
bruno init sample-api
```

Here, Bruno responds by creating a directory structure tailored for our API development. We see directories for endpoints, configuration files, and a default script file.

Running Sample Script

Next, we want to test our environment by running a sample script. Assume we have created a simple script named **`hello.bru`** that defines a basic endpoint:

```
// hello.bru
```

```
endpoint /greet {
  method: GET;
  response: {
    status: 200;
    body: "Greetings from Bruno!"
  }
}
```

We run the script with:

```
bruno run hello.bru
```

The terminal outputs confirmation that the **`/greet`** endpoint has been registered successfully. This immediate feedback reinforces our confidence in Bruno's ability to process our commands accurately.

Viewing Project Status

To ensure that our project is functioning as expected, we check the status:

```
bruno status
```

The output provides a summary of active endpoints and running processes, confirming that our API environment is set up correctly.

Exploring Configuration

Finally, we verify that our configuration is active by reviewing the current settings:

```
bruno config --show
```

This command displays our current configuration, confirming that our earlier setup for Bru Lang and Bruno CLI remains in effect.

Now that we've got a handle on Bruno's interface and command structure, it's time to take things a step further and dive into the world of API development. Each command we execute now feels like it's in line with a streamlined and efficient workflow.

Summary

So, in this chapter, we got to use Bruno. We learned how its capabilities are there every step of the way, from the initial design to debugging and performance monitoring. We also saw some practical examples of how Bruno's features make it easy to create API endpoints, model request and response structures, and integrate business logic. We installed the Bruno command-line interface (CLI) and configured Bru Lang in our Linux environment using clear, step-by-step commands, making sure our tools were set up for advanced development tasks.

We also explored Bruno's interface and command structure, discovering intuitive commands that let us easily initiate projects, run scripts, and manage configurations. We found that using commands like bruno init, bruno run, and bruno config really streamlined our development process and made it more consistent. This chapter made us feel more confident and gave us a better understanding of Bruno while knowing that postman and insomnia are well developed in the domain of API development.

CHAPTER 2: STRUCTURING API PROJECT

Overview

Now, in this chapter, we're going to lay out the structure of our API project. We'll start by mapping out its architecture and defining the key elements that form its backbone. First, we'll outline the overall API structure, identify the endpoints that'll be our interaction points, and establish a clear blueprint that details the flow of data. Then, we'll move on to defining specific endpoints and constructing detailed data schemas that ensure consistency and accuracy in both requests and responses. We'll set up naming conventions, decide on the right HTTP methods, and design the URL structure for each endpoint.

We'll also explore techniques for modeling complex request payloads that include nested objects, arrays, and optional fields, as well as crafting robust response structures that handle both successful interactions and error scenarios. Through hands-on examples using Bru Lang, we'll show you how to implement these concepts in our Linux environment, providing a solid foundation for future development phases. This chapter's going to get us prepared to build a strong and flexible API, so we can be confident in extending and maintaining the project as new requirements pop up.

Mapping API Structure

A well-defined blueprint ensures that every endpoint has a purpose, the data it expects is validated, and the output is predictable. The blueprint is not only a design document but also serves as a working reference for the entire API development process. So here, we start by sketching a high-level overview that includes endpoint naming conventions, the structure of input data, and the format of responses that our API will deliver.

For instance, we may decide that our API follows RESTful principles, where each endpoint corresponds to a specific resource or action. The structure will include endpoints for user management, data retrieval, and action triggers. As we proceed, every endpoint will be defined with its HTTP method, the expected request payload, and the resulting response structure.

Modeling Endpoints

Establishing Endpoint Conventions

When we model endpoints, it is important to follow naming conventions that are both descriptive and consistent. For our Lumina API project, we might choose endpoint names that clearly indicate the function they perform.

For example, endpoints could be structured as follows:

- **GET /users**: Retrieves a list of users.
- **POST /users**: Creates a new user.

- **GET /users/{id}**: Fetches details of a specific user.
- **PUT /users/{id}**: Updates the information for a specific user.
- **DELETE /users/{id}**: Removes a specific user.

When the endpoints are well defined, we reduce the risk of misinterpretation and minimize the effort required for future modifications.

Sample Endpoint

We will consider a practical example for the endpoint that creates a new user. In our project, this endpoint might be modeled in Bru Lang using a syntax that is both simple and expressive.

So, a sample definition might look like this:

```
endpoint /users {
  method: POST;
  request: {
    body: {
      username: string,
      email: string,
      password: string
    }
  };
  response: {
    status: 201,
    body: {
      id: number,
      username: string,
      email: string,
      createdAt: datetime
    }
  }
}
```

In this definition, we clearly specify that the **`/users`** endpoint uses the POST method, expects a request payload with fields like username, email, and password, and returns a response containing the new user's details. This modular approach allows us to later extend or modify the endpoint without impacting other parts of our API.

Designing Request Payloads

The next step in mapping our API structure is to model the request payloads. Request payloads are the data we send to our API endpoints to perform actions or create resources. In our Lumina API project, we will use a clear JSON schema to represent the data. The schema will define the expected data types, required fields, and any constraints on the data.

For example, when creating a new user, the request payload might be structured as follows:

```
{
  "username": "john_doe",
  "email": "john@gitforgits.com",
  "password": "securePassword123"
}
```

In our blueprint, we specify that the payload must include a username as a string, an email formatted as a string, and a password also as a string. This level of detail minimizes errors during processing and allows us to implement robust validation mechanisms within Bruno.

Designing Response Structures

Defining Output Formats

Once we have modeled our endpoints and request payloads, our next focus is on designing the response structures. Responses are what our API returns after processing a request, and they need to be structured to provide clear and actionable data. In our project, each response is modeled using a JSON schema that specifies the status code, headers, and the body of the response.

For instance, a successful user creation might return a response with a status code of 201, along with details of the newly created user as shown below:

```
{
  "id": 101,
  "username": "john_doe",
  "email": "john@gitforgits.com",
  "createdAt": "2024-04-27T12:34:56Z"
```

```
}
```

This consistency improves readability and also simplifies error handling and integration with front-end applications.

Integrating Error Handling into Responses

In addition to successful responses, it is critical that our API structure accommodates error responses. Error responses provide feedback when something goes wrong, such as when a request payload is missing required fields or contains invalid data. In our blueprint, we include error response definitions that follow a similar JSON schema, ensuring consistency across all endpoints.

A typical error response might look like this:

```
{
  "error": "InvalidRequest",
  "message": "The 'email' field is required.",
  "code": 400
}
```

This structure makes it clear to the API consumer what went wrong, while also providing a standard format that can be handled programmatically by client applications.

Throughout the above whole mapping process, we did see that each defined endpoint, payload, and response plays a role in constructing an API that is both reliable and scalable. This systematic approach also simplifies collaboration, as every team member can refer to the same blueprint, reducing misunderstandings and ensuring that every part of the API is aligned with the overall project vision.

Defining Endpoints and Data Schema

When designing an API, endpoints serve as the communication touchpoints through which clients interact with our service. Each endpoint represents a resource or an action that can be performed on that resource. The data schema, on the other hand, defines the structure of the request payloads and responses. It ensures that the data transmitted to and from these endpoints is validated, consistent, and well-formed. For our Lumina API project, we plan to follow RESTful conventions as a starting point, though the principles can be applied to other architectural styles. The endpoints will be designed to handle operations such as creating resources, retrieving information, updating existing records, and deleting entries. In tandem, our data schemas will be defined to validate input from clients and ensure that our responses maintain a predictable structure. The patterns we set here will be the reference point for every future development step in the project.

Process of Defining Endpoints

But before we start coding, we need to understand the goal for each endpoint. So, first we'll list the key features our API should support. For the Lumina project, we've identified a few core functionalities like user management, session handling, data retrieval, and logging operations.

For example, endpoints will be created for tasks like:

- Creating a new user account.
- Retrieving user details.
- Updating user information.
- Deleting a user account.
- Fetching a list of users.

This above initial planning phase helps in assigning the correct HTTP methods (GET, POST, PUT, DELETE) to each operation and guides the structure of our data schemas.

Now when you are busy in defining endpoints, several practical aspects must be taken into account, such as:

- **HTTP Methods**: Each endpoint is associated with an HTTP method that indicates the type of operation being performed. For instance, GET is used for data retrieval without side effects, while POST is typically used for creating new resources.
- **URL Structure**: The URL structure should be hierarchical and intuitive. For example, nested resources can be represented with URLs like **`/users/{id}/posts`** for posts made by a specific user.
- **Versioning**: Although not immediately implemented, it is wise to consider how versioning will be managed. Including versioning in the URL (e.g., **`/v1/users`**) can simplify future updates.
- **Error Handling**: Each endpoint should define a clear response schema not only for successful operations but also for error conditions. This includes HTTP status codes and a structured error message that can be used by client applications to handle failures gracefully.

While security configuration is handled separately, endpoints should also be designed with access controls in mind. This means that endpoints handling sensitive data may have additional constraints or require specific authorization tokens.

Constructing Data Schemas

Schemas are like the building blocks of data. They define the structure and type of data that an

API expects as input and returns as output. They're basically a blueprint for both request payloads and response bodies. A well-designed schema includes definitions for data types (like strings, numbers, booleans, and objects), mandatory fields, default values, and constraints like maximum lengths or pattern restrictions. In our project, data schemas make sure that every API call is validated against expected formats, reducing the risk of malformed data reaching our backend systems.

To ensure the schemas are robust, several best practices can be followed such as:

- **Explicit Field Definitions**: Every field in the schema should have an explicit data type and, if applicable, a description that indicates its purpose.
- **Required vs. Optional Fields**: Clearly mark which fields are required for the operation to succeed, and which fields are optional.
- **Nested Structures**: For complex data, nested objects or arrays can be used to represent the structure. For example, an address might be a nested object within a user profile.
- **Version Control**: Maintain schema versions so that any changes to the data structure over time can be tracked and managed.
- **Validation Rules**: Incorporate validation rules directly into the schema definition to enforce constraints, such as the format of an email address or the minimum length of a password.

While we define our schemas within our API blueprint using Bru Lang, it is helpful to be aware of other schema definition languages like JSON Schema.

Sample Program: Defining Endpoints and Data Schemas

You'll be able to put theory into practice here by defining endpoints and data schemas for the Lumina API project using Bru Lang. The examples below show how to write these definitions in a clear and modular manner. We'll start by defining a couple of key endpoints for user management, including the creation of a new user and retrieving a user's details.

Defining "Create User" Endpoint

The "Create User" endpoint is designed to accept a POST request with a JSON payload containing the new user's details. The response will confirm the creation of the user along with a unique identifier and other relevant information.

Below is a sample definition written in Bru Lang:

```
// Define the endpoint for creating a new user
endpoint /users {
  method: POST;
```

```
  // Define the structure for the request payload
  request: {
    body: {
      username: string,        // The unique username for the
new user
      email: string,           // The email address, which must
be valid
      password: string         // A secure password that meets
complexity requirements
    }
  };
  // Define the structure for the response body
  response: {
    status: 201;
    body: {
      id: number,              // The unique identifier for the
newly created user
      username: string,        // The username of the created
user
      email: string,           // The registered email address
      createdAt: datetime      // Timestamp indicating when the
user was created
    }
  };
  // Define error responses for common issues
  error: {
    400: {
      error: "InvalidInput",
      message: "Missing or invalid fields in the request
payload."
    },
```

```
    409: {
      error: "UserExists",
      message: "A user with the provided email or username
already exists."
    }
  }
}
```

In the above program, we clearly define what the API expects and returns. The request body requires three fields: **`username`**, **`email`**, and **`password`**, all of which are marked with their respective data types. The response is designed to return a status code of 201 upon success, along with a JSON object containing the new user's ID, username, email, and creation timestamp.

Defining "Retrieve User Details" Endpoint

The next endpoint we define is for retrieving user details using a GET request. This endpoint expects an identifier as a path parameter and returns the corresponding user information.

Following is the definition for it:

```
// Define the endpoint for retrieving user details
endpoint /users/{id} {
  method: GET;
  // Define the structure for the request parameters
  request: {
    params: {
      id: number           // The unique identifier for the
user to be retrieved
    }
  };
  // Define the structure for the response body
  response: {
    status: 200;
    body: {
```

```
      id: number,           // The unique identifier for the
user
      username: string,     // The username of the user
      email: string,        // The registered email address
      createdAt: datetime   // Timestamp indicating when the
user was created
    }
  };
  // Define error responses for scenarios like not found
  error: {
    404: {
      error: "NotFound",
      message: "User not found with the given identifier."
    }
  }
}
```

The above definition makes use of path parameters to capture the user ID. The response is structured to include all necessary details of the user, and a clear error response is provided for cases when the user is not found.

Additional Endpoints

For a robust API, it is common to include endpoints for updating and deleting resources as shown below:

```
// Define the endpoint for updating user information
endpoint /users/{id} {
  method: PUT;
  // Define the structure for the request payload and
parameters
  request: {
    params: {
```

```
      id: number           // The unique identifier for the
user to be updated
    },
    body: {
      username: string?,    // Optional: New username, if
updating
      email: string?,       // Optional: New email address, if
updating
      password: string?     // Optional: New password, if
updating
    }
  };
  // Define the structure for the response body
  response: {
    status: 200;
    body: {
      id: number,           // The unique identifier for the
updated user
      username: string,     // The updated username
      email: string,        // The updated email address
      updatedAt: datetime   // Timestamp indicating when the
update occurred
    }
  };
  // Define error responses
  error: {
    400: {
      error: "InvalidInput",
      message: "Provided data for update is invalid."
    },
    404: {
```

```
      error: "NotFound",
      message: "User not found for the given identifier."
    }
  }
}
```

In this definition, we incorporate optional fields in the request payload by marking them as optional with a question mark (**?**). This allows flexibility in the update operation, as the client may choose to update one or more attributes of the user. The response includes an **`updatedAt`** timestamp to indicate when the changes were applied.

Below is how we define another endpoint for deleting a user:

```
// Define the endpoint for deleting a user
endpoint /users/{id} {
  method: DELETE;
  // Define the structure for the request parameters
  request: {
    params: {
      id: number             // The unique identifier for the
user to be deleted
    }
  };
  // Define the structure for the response body
  response: {
    status: 204;             // No content returned for a
successful deletion
    body: {}                 // An empty body indicates that the
deletion was successful
  };
  // Define error responses for deletion failures
  error: {
    404: {
```

```
      error: "NotFound",
      message: "User not found for the provided identifier."
    }
  }
}
```

Here, the DELETE operation returns a status code of 204, signifying that the resource has been removed and no further content is necessary in the response body.

Constructing Data Schemas in Detail

Detailed Schema Definition for User Resource

A well-defined data schema for our user resource ensures that the data transmitted between the client and server is both valid and predictable. For the Lumina project, we will adopt a JSON-based schema definition that can be integrated directly into our endpoint definitions.

Below is a detailed schema for the user resource:

```
{
  "type": "object",
  "properties": {
    "id": {
      "type": "number",
      "description": "A unique identifier for the user, auto-
generated by the system."
    },
    "username": {
      "type": "string",
      "minLength": 3,
      "maxLength": 30,
      "description": "The unique username chosen by the user."
    },
    "email": {
      "type": "string",
```

```
      "format": "email",
      "description": "The user's email address."
    },
    "password": {
      "type": "string",
      "minLength": 8,
      "description": "A secure password that meets complexity
requirements."
    },
    "createdAt": {
      "type": "string",
      "format": "date-time",
      "description": "The timestamp when the user was
created."
    },
    "updatedAt": {
      "type": "string",
      "format": "date-time",
      "description": "The timestamp when the user details were
last updated."
    }
  },
  "required": ["username", "email", "password"]
}
```

This schema precisely defines what the user object should contain. It includes data types, formats, and constraints, ensuring that all incoming and outgoing data adhere to this structure. The required fields ensure that essential data is always provided, while optional fields like **`updatedAt`** allow for flexibility during updates.

Integrating Schema Validation

For each endpoint, when a request is received, Bruno validates the payload against the corresponding schema. This validation step is critical in preventing malformed data from entering our application logic. In our project, we rely on these validations to ensure that the data for operations such as user creation or update adheres to our strict requirements.

So to illustrate this, let us go back to the "Create User" endpoint defined earlier. When a POST request is made to **/users**, Bruno uses the user schema to validate that the **username**, **email**, and **password** fields are present and correctly formatted. If the validation fails, the system automatically returns a structured error response as defined in our endpoint configuration.

Using Schema Definitions across Endpoints

Since it's a best practice in API development to define reusable schema components that can be referenced across multiple endpoints, our user schema can be used in the "Create User" endpoint as well as endpoints for updating or retrieving user details. This reuse of schemas minimizes redundancy and maintains consistency throughout the API.

In our Bru Lang configuration, we might define the user schema as a reusable component:

```
// Define reusable user schema
schema User {
  id: number,
  username: string,
  email: string,
  password: string,
  createdAt: datetime,
  updatedAt: datetime?
}
```

With this schema defined once, endpoints can reference **User** directly, ensuring that any changes to the schema propagate automatically to all dependent endpoints. For example, the "Retrieve User Details" endpoint can reference the **User** schema in its response definition. This whole modular approach ensures that any changes to the schema or endpoint logic can be managed centrally by and among team members.

Request and Response Structures

Before diving into the code, it is important to recognize that APIs often handle data that is more intricate than simple key-value pairs. In real-world scenarios, requests and responses may involve nested objects, arrays, conditional fields, and even polymorphic data. Our objective is to define these structures in a way that makes it easy for both the API provider and consumer to understand the data exchange. This approach minimizes errors and improves overall communication between systems. By carefully modeling these complex formats, we not only create a reliable interface but also simplify the integration and troubleshooting processes later on.

Modeling Complex Request Structures

Handling Nested Objects

A common scenario is when a request contains nested objects. For example, a user registration endpoint requires basic user information and also details related to the user's profile. This profile information may include an address, contact details, or even social media links. In Bru Lang, we define nested objects to represent these hierarchies clearly.

An example request payload for creating a new user with nested profile details might look like as shown below:

```
endpoint /users {
  method: POST;
  request: {
    body: {
      username: string,
      email: string,
      password: string,
      profile: {
        firstName: string,
        lastName: string,
        address: {
          street: string,
          city: string,
          postalCode: string,
          country: string
        },
        contacts: [
          {
```

```
          type: string,
          number: string
        }
      ]
    }
  }
};
response: {
  status: 201,
  body: {
    id: number,
    username: string,
    email: string,
    createdAt: datetime
  }
}
}
```

In this definition, the request body contains a **`profile`** object that itself contains another nested **`address`** object and an array of **`contacts`**. This layered structure helps us to send detailed and organized data in a single request.

Incorporating Optional Fields and Conditional Data

Often, certain fields in a request may not always be applicable. For example, a user might choose to provide social media information only if available. Using optional fields allows us to design requests that are both flexible and robust. In our request definitions, we mark these fields as optional. This might be done using a specific notation (such as a question mark) to indicate that the field may or may not be present as shown below:

```
endpoint /users {
  method: POST;
  request: {
    body: {
```

```
      username: string,
      email: string,
      password: string,
      profile: {
        firstName: string,
        lastName: string,
        address: {
          street: string,
          city: string,
          postalCode: string,
          country: string
        },
        contacts: [
          {
            type: string,
            number: string
          }
        ],
        socialMedia?: {
          twitter: string?,
          facebook: string?,
          instagram: string?
        }
      }
    }
  };
  response: {
    status: 201,
    body: {
```

```
        id: number,
        username: string,
        email: string,
        createdAt: datetime
      }
    }
  }
```

In the above script, the **socialMedia** field is optional and can include optional entries for Twitter, Facebook, or Instagram.

Representing Arrays in Requests

In our Lumina API, arrays can be used to represent multiple items, such as a list of contact numbers or a set of preferences. When modeling arrays, it is important to define the data type of the items they contain.

So for instance, if we need to capture multiple email addresses or tags, we define the array as follows:

```
endpoint /users {
  method: POST;
  request: {
    body: {
      username: string,
      email: string,
      password: string,
      tags: [string]  // An array of strings representing
user-defined tags
    }
  };
  response: {
    status: 201,
    body: {
```

```
            id: number,
            username: string,
            email: string,
            tags: [string],
            createdAt: datetime
        }
    }
}
```

This definition clarifies that the **`tags`** field is an array consisting solely of strings, ensuring that our API correctly interprets the data structure.

Modeling Complex Response Structures

Designing Rich Response Objects

When the API processes a request, it often returns more detailed information than simply a success status. For example, a GET request retrieving user details may include nested data, aggregated statistics, or metadata. The rich response objects improve clarity and assist clients in understanding the outcome of their requests.

So to understand better, we will assess an example where the response contains nested objects and arrays to deliver comprehensive user data:

```
endpoint /users/{id} {
    method: GET;
    request: {
        params: {
            id: number
        }
    };
    response: {
        status: 200,
        body: {
            id: number,
```

```
    username: string,
    email: string,
    profile: {
      firstName: string,
      lastName: string,
      address: {
        street: string,
        city: string,
        postalCode: string,
        country: string
      },
      contacts: [
        {
          type: string,
          number: string
        }
      ]
    },
    settings: {
      preferences: [string],
      notifications: boolean
    },
    createdAt: datetime
  }
};
error: {
  404: {
    error: "NotFound",
    message: "User not found with the given identifier."
```

```
    }
  }
}
```

Here, the response body is designed to provide a full picture of the user, including their profile with nested address and contacts, as well as additional settings like preferences and notification status. This detailed response ensures that the client receives all necessary information in one structured format.

Handling Pagination and Metadata

For endpoints that return lists of resources, such as retrieving all users, we need to include pagination and metadata in the response. It helps to manage large datasets and provides context about the result set as shown below:

```
endpoint /users {
  method: GET;
  request: {
    query: {
      page: number,
      limit: number
    }
  };
  response: {
    status: 200,
    body: {
      data: [
        {
          id: number,
          username: string,
          email: string,
          createdAt: datetime
        }
      ],
```

```
      meta: {
        totalCount: number,
        page: number,
        limit: number
      }
    }
  };
  error: {
    400: {
      error: "InvalidQuery",
      message: "Query parameters for pagination are invalid."
    }
  }
}
```

In the above script, the response body includes a **data** array that holds the actual user records and a **meta** object that provides pagination details.

Standardizing Error Responses

Errors are a normal part of complex systems, and it's essential to have a standard way of dealing with them. Our approach is to use a consistent format for all error messages across different endpoints. An error response typically includes an error code, a message, and sometimes extra details that help identify and fix the issue as shown below:

```
error: {
  400: {
    error: "BadRequest",
    message: "The provided input does not meet the required
schema."
  },
  404: {
    error: "NotFound",
```

```
    message: "The requested resource could not be found."
  },
  500: {
    error: "InternalError",
    message: "An unexpected error occurred on the server."
  }
}
```

By standardizing error responses, we ensure that every endpoint returns errors in a predictable format, which simplifies error handling on the client side.

Implementing Complex Structures

To effectively model request and response structures in our Lumina API, we combine the techniques learned above. This includes handling nested objects, optional fields, arrays, and metadata. The following example illustrates a holistic endpoint that leverages these concepts:

```
// Comprehensive endpoint for user creation with detailed
profile and settings
endpoint /users {
  method: POST;
  request: {
    body: {
      username: string,
      email: string,
      password: string,
      profile: {
        firstName: string,
        lastName: string,
        address: {
          street: string,
          city: string,
          postalCode: string,
```

```
        country: string
      },
      contacts: [
        {
          type: string,
          number: string
        }
      ],
      socialMedia?: {
        twitter: string?,
        facebook: string?,
        instagram: string?
      }
    },
    settings: {
      preferences: [string],
      notifications: boolean
    }
  }
};
response: {
  status: 201,
  body: {
    id: number,
    username: string,
    email: string,
    profile: {
      firstName: string,
      lastName: string,
```

```
      address: {
        street: string,
        city: string,
        postalCode: string,
        country: string
      },
      contacts: [
        {
          type: string,
          number: string
        }
      ],
      socialMedia?: {
        twitter: string?,
        facebook: string?,
        instagram: string?
      }
    },
    settings: {
      preferences: [string],
      notifications: boolean
    },
    createdAt: datetime
  }
};
error: {
  400: {
    error: "InvalidInput",
```

```
      message: "Required fields are missing or contain invalid
data."
    },
    409: {
      error: "UserExists",
      message: "A user with the provided email or username
already exists."
    }
  }
}
```

The endpoint clearly defines what data is expected in the request, how it is structured, and what the response will look like. This cohesive approach maintains consistency and reliability in our API that helps both developers and clients to interact with the system.

Summary

At the start of this chapter, we built on our initial framework by defining endpoints and constructing comprehensive data schemas for our Lumina API project. We began by figuring out the basic functions our API was designed to perform, like creating, retrieving, updating, and deleting user records. We set up clear naming conventions and logical URL structures that made it so operations flowed smoothly. We also used best practices, like using HTTP methods, query parameters, and path variables, to reduce confusion in the API.

Then, we figured out how to handle complex request payloads with nested objects, arrays, and optional fields, so we could get all the user info in one go. At the same time, we came up with solid response formats that gave us the data we needed and clear error messages to deal with any problems. We also tested these models with simulated API calls to make sure every endpoint met our standards for data integrity and usability. By the end of the chapter, we had set up a reliable contract between client and server, and our detailed API structure was a solid base for more improvements and integrations in the Lumina API project. This whole process really improved our overall development workflow.

Chapter 3: Designing API Project

Overview

In this chapter, we will design the Lumina API project by defining clear specifications that cover both functional and non-functional requirements. We will outline every aspect of our API, from the essential operations like user registration, retrieval, updating, and deletion, to the finer details of session handling and data validation. We will also create detailed API blueprints that visually map out our endpoints and data flows, using Bruno's syntax to translate our ideas into practical, executable code.

Furthermore, we will implement version control practices to track modifications and manage changes systematically, ensuring that our design evolves in a controlled and predictable manner. Collaborative documentation techniques will also be introduced, allowing us to maintain a single source of truth for our API specifications and share insights among team members seamlessly.

Establishing API Specifications

To start, we'll lay out the requirements that are functional and those that aren't, create solid data contracts, and document how things should interact. These specs will be the plan for every development phase in Bruno in order to ensure the project's operational and functional needs are clear and can be put into action.

Functional Requirements

For the Lumina project, we will establish a set of concrete functional requirements that define what the API must accomplish. The API will primarily manage user accounts, support session handling, and provide a means for data retrieval and update.

The specific functional requirements include:

- **User Registration**
  - The API must allow the creation of new user accounts.
  - A unique username and a valid email address will be required.
  - The password must meet defined complexity rules (minimum 8 characters with a mix of uppercase, lowercase, and digits).
  - Upon successful registration, the API should return a unique user identifier and timestamp.
- **User Retrieval**
  - The API must allow retrieval of user details using a unique identifier.
  - The response should include all relevant user data such as username, email, profile information, and account creation date.

    - It should also support fetching lists of users with pagination parameters.
- **User Update**
    - The API should allow updating user information, including optional fields such as a profile picture, social media links, or contact numbers.
    - Only valid and authenticated requests must be allowed to update sensitive fields like email or password.
    - The API should return the updated user details along with a new timestamp indicating the update.
- **User Deletion**
    - The API must support the deletion of a user account given a valid identifier.
    - Upon deletion, the API should confirm the removal with an appropriate status code and an empty response body.
- **Session Management**
    - The API will support session handling by allowing users to log in and out.
    - On login, a session token should be generated and returned.
    - The API must also provide endpoints to validate and invalidate session tokens.

Non-Functional Requirements

In addition to functional requirements, the Lumina project specifications include important non-functional requirements to ensure the API is robust, efficient, and secure:

- **Performance**
    - The API should respond to user registration and login requests within 200 milliseconds under normal load.
    - Pagination endpoints should return results promptly even when handling large data sets (e.g., up to 10,000 records).
- **Scalability**
    - The API must be designed to support horizontal scaling, with clear guidelines on how endpoints will behave under increased traffic.
    - It should handle concurrent requests without data integrity issues.
- **Security**
    - All endpoints must enforce secure communication protocols (HTTPS).
    - Sensitive information such as passwords must be hashed using industry-standard

algorithms before storage.
    - Session tokens must be encrypted and have a defined expiry time to prevent unauthorized access.
- **Error Handling and Reliability**
    - The API must provide standardized error responses for invalid requests, resource conflicts, or internal server errors.
    - Logging should be integrated to capture error details and facilitate rapid debugging.
    - The API will include automated monitoring to alert developers if response times exceed predefined thresholds.
- **Maintainability**
    - The API must follow RESTful best practices with consistent naming conventions and URL structures.
    - Data contracts should be versioned to allow smooth transitions during updates.
    - The codebase and configuration files should be well-documented to assist future developers.

Data Contracts and Schema Definitions

A key aspect of our API specifications is the establishment of precise data contracts. These contracts define the structure of data exchanged between the client and server to have consistency and reliability across all endpoints.

For the user management functionality, we will define a JSON schema that captures all necessary user attributes. The schema is defined as follows:

```
{
  "type": "object",
  "properties": {
    "id": {
      "type": "number",
      "description": "Auto-generated unique identifier for the
user."
    },
    "username": {
      "type": "string",
```

```
      "minLength": 3,
      "maxLength": 30,
      "description": "A unique username chosen by the user."
    },
    "email": {
      "type": "string",
      "format": "email",
      "description": "The user's valid email address."
    },
    "password": {
      "type": "string",
      "minLength": 8,
      "description": "A secure password that meets complexity
requirements."
    },
    "profile": {
      "type": "object",
      "properties": {
        "firstName": { "type": "string" },
        "lastName": { "type": "string" },
        "address": {
          "type": "object",
          "properties": {
            "street": { "type": "string" },
            "city": { "type": "string" },
            "postalCode": { "type": "string" },
            "country": { "type": "string" }
          },
          "required": ["street", "city", "postalCode",
"country"]
```

```
        },
        "contacts": {
          "type": "array",
          "items": {
            "type": "object",
            "properties": {
              "type": { "type": "string" },
              "number": { "type": "string" }
            },
            "required": ["type", "number"]
          }
        }
      },
      "required": ["firstName", "lastName", "address"]
    },
    "createdAt": {
      "type": "string",
      "format": "date-time",
      "description": "Timestamp when the user was created."
    },
    "updatedAt": {
      "type": "string",
      "format": "date-time",
      "description": "Timestamp when the user was last
updated."
    }
  },
  "required": ["username", "email", "password", "profile"]
}
```

This schema confirms that every user record is consistent, and it enforces key validations such as email format and password length. The nested objects within the **`profile`** property allow us to capture detailed user information, and arrays such as **`contacts`** facilitate multiple entries without compromising the overall structure.

Documenting Interaction Patterns

Now here, to complement our functional and data specifications, we need to document the typical interaction patterns between the client and the API. These patterns describe how requests are made, how data flows through the system, and what responses are expected under different scenarios.

Registration and Authentication Flow

For instance, the user registration flow will follow these steps:

- A POST request is sent to **`/users`** with a payload adhering to the defined user schema.
- Upon successful validation, the API responds with a 201 status code, including the newly generated **`id`** and **`createdAt`** timestamp.
- If the username or email already exists, a 409 error with a descriptive message is returned.

Similarly, the user login will be followed as:

- A POST request is sent to **`/login`** (or a similar authentication endpoint) with credentials.
- The API verifies the credentials and returns a session token with a 200 status code.
- Invalid credentials result in a 401 error with an appropriate error message.

Data Retrieval and Update Patterns

For data retrieval and update, the interaction pattern is similarly defined:

- To retrieve data, a GET request to **`/users/{id}`** returns detailed user information along with metadata.
- The response structure adheres to the user schema, ensuring consistency across different endpoints.
- For data update, a PUT request to **`/users/{id}`** is used for updating user details.
- The request payload may include optional fields, and the API responds with updated user details along with an **`updatedAt`** timestamp.

Once we've got our data contracts and interaction patterns set up in the Bruno setup, every endpoint will behave just how we want it to. The config files will include references to our JSON schemas and enforce validation rules at runtime. So, if the data structure doesn't match what we expect, it'll trigger immediate feedback, which'll let us make corrections during development.

Creating Detailed API Blueprints

The first step in creating our API blueprints is to outline the overall architecture of the Lumina API. This involves mapping out all primary endpoints and defining their relationships, which include user registration, data retrieval, updates, deletions, and session management. Our goal is to visualize and have a reference of how data flows between different parts of the API. The blueprint must be modular, so that each endpoint can be developed and maintained independently, yet function seamlessly as part of the whole system.

So, before we write any code, we establish a high-level map of endpoints:

- **/users (POST):** Create a new user.
- **/users/{id} (GET):** Retrieve user details.
- **/users/{id} (PUT):** Update user information.
- **/users/{id} (DELETE):** Delete a user.
- **/login (POST):** Manage user authentication.
- **/logout (POST):** Invalidate an active session.
- **/sessions (GET):** Retrieve session details for monitoring purposes.

This high-level map provides us with a clear overview of the actions our API must support. We then incorporate data flow elements that define how the data moves through these endpoints—from the request payload to processing logic and ultimately to the response.

Drafting Endpoints Using Bruno's Syntax

Using Bruno's declarative syntax, we now begin drafting the blueprints for each endpoint. Each blueprint includes sections for the HTTP method, request parameters, request body schema, and response structure. The code examples below illustrate how the blueprint is constructed for key endpoints in the Lumina API.

User Registration Blueprint

The first endpoint we define handles user registration. This endpoint will accept a POST request, validate the input against our user schema, and return the new user's details.

```
// Blueprint for user registration
endpoint /users {
```

```
  method: POST;
  request: {
    body: {
      username: string,          // Unique username (3-30
characters)
      email: string,             // Valid email address
      password: string,          // Secure password (min 8
characters)
      profile: {                 // Nested profile details
        firstName: string,
        lastName: string,
        address: {
          street: string,
          city: string,
          postalCode: string,
          country: string
        },
        contacts: [
          {
            type: string,
            number: string
          }
        ],
        socialMedia?: {          // Optional social media handles
          twitter: string?,
          facebook: string?,
          instagram: string?
        }
      },
      settings: {                // User-specific settings
```

```
          preferences: [string],
          notifications: boolean
        }
      }
    };
    response: {
      status: 201;
      body: {
        id: number,                // Auto-generated unique user
identifier
        username: string,
        email: string,
        profile: {
          firstName: string,
          lastName: string,
          address: {
            street: string,
            city: string,
            postalCode: string,
            country: string
          },
          contacts: [
            {
              type: string,
              number: string
            }
          ],
          socialMedia?: {         // Optional social media data
            twitter: string?,
```

```
          facebook: string?,
          instagram: string?
        }
      },
      settings: {
        preferences: [string],
        notifications: boolean
      },
      createdAt: datetime     // Timestamp of user creation
    }
  };
  error: {
    400: {
      error: "InvalidInput",
      message: "Required fields are missing or contain invalid
data."
    },
    409: {
      error: "UserExists",
      message: "A user with the provided email or username
already exists."
    }
  }
}
```

This blueprint clearly defines how the registration process is expected to work. The request body is comprehensive, including nested objects for profile and settings, while the response confirms the creation with a unique ID and a timestamp.

User Retrieval Blueprint

Next, we define the blueprint for retrieving user details. This endpoint uses a GET request and relies on a path parameter to identify the user.

```
// Blueprint for retrieving user details
endpoint /users/{id} {
  method: GET;
  request: {
    params: {
      id: number              // The unique identifier of the
user
    }
  };
  response: {
    status: 200;
    body: {
      id: number,
      username: string,
      email: string,
      profile: {
        firstName: string,
        lastName: string,
        address: {
          street: string,
          city: string,
          postalCode: string,
          country: string
        },
        contacts: [
          {
            type: string,
            number: string
          }
```

```
        ],
        socialMedia?: {         // Optional social media handles
          twitter: string?,
          facebook: string?,
          instagram: string?
        }
      },
      settings: {
        preferences: [string],
        notifications: boolean
      },
      createdAt: datetime       // Timestamp of creation
    }
  };
  error: {
    404: {
      error: "NotFound",
      message: "User not found with the given identifier."
    }
  }
}
```

This blueprint emphasizes the importance of path parameters for targeted retrieval. The response structure mirrors the user registration response to maintain consistency.

User Update Blueprint

To update user information, you need a flexible endpoint that can handle optional fields. The following blueprint shows how this endpoint accepts partial updates while enforcing validation on critical fields.

```
// Blueprint for updating user information
endpoint /users/{id} {
```

```
  method: PUT;
  request: {
    params: {
      id: number            // The unique identifier for the
user to be updated
    },
    body: {
      username: string?,     // Optional update of username
      email: string?,        // Optional update of email
      password: string?,     // Optional update of password
      profile: {             // Update profile details if
provided
        firstName: string?,
        lastName: string?,
        address: {
          street: string?,
          city: string?,
          postalCode: string?,
          country: string?
        },
        contacts: [
          {
            type: string,
            number: string
          }
        ]?,
        socialMedia?: {        // Optional social media updates
          twitter: string?,
          facebook: string?,
          instagram: string?
```

```
      }
    }?,
    settings: {             // Optional updates for user
settings
      preferences: [string]?,
      notifications: boolean?
    }?
  }
};
response: {
  status: 200;
  body: {
    id: number,
    username: string,
    email: string,
    profile: {
      firstName: string,
      lastName: string,
      address: {
        street: string,
        city: string,
        postalCode: string,
        country: string
      },
      contacts: [
        {
          type: string,
          number: string
        }
```

```
        ],
        socialMedia?: {       // Updated social media details
if provided
          twitter: string?,
          facebook: string?,
          instagram: string?
        }
      },
      settings: {
        preferences: [string],
        notifications: boolean
      },
      updatedAt: datetime    // Timestamp indicating the time
of update
    }
  };
  error: {
    400: {
      error: "InvalidInput",
      message: "Provided data for update is invalid."
    },
    404: {
      error: "NotFound",
      message: "User not found for the given identifier."
    }
  }
}
```

The update blueprint supports partial updates by marking fields as optional. With this, users can modify only the information they choose to change without needing to resend the entire user object.

User Deletion Blueprint

For deletion, we focus upon validating the user identifier and confirming the removal of the resource.

```
// Blueprint for deleting a user
endpoint /users/{id} {
  method: DELETE;
  request: {
    params: {
      id: number                // The unique identifier for the
user to be deleted
    }
  };
  response: {
    status: 204;                // No content returned for a
successful deletion
    body: {}                    // Empty body to signify successful
deletion
  };
  error: {
    404: {
      error: "NotFound",
      message: "User not found for the provided identifier."
    }
  }
}
```

The deletion blueprint is straightforward, providing a clear signal to the client that the operation has been successful through a 204 status code and an empty response body.

Data Flow and Interaction Patterns

The blueprints serve not only as code definitions but also as a roadmap for how data moves through the system. Each endpoint enforces a contract that dictates:

- **Input Validation**

  Data received in the request body or as parameters is validated against predefined schemas. Any deviation results in a structured error response resulting in data integrity from the start.

- **Processing Logic**

  Once data is validated, the processing logic (not detailed in the blueprints but implemented in the application layer) handles business rules, such as checking for duplicate users, hashing passwords, and updating timestamps.

- **Response Generation**

  Successful processing results in a structured response that adheres strictly to the defined schema. This response includes all relevant metadata, such as unique identifiers and timestamps, to inform the client of the operation's outcome.

- **Error Handling**

  Each endpoint blueprint includes error definitions, such that every possible failure, like invalid input or missing resources, is met with a predictable error format that clients can handle programmatically.

Once the individual endpoint blueprints are drafted, they are integrated into the overall project structure. In the Lumina API project, these blueprints are organized in dedicated files within a structured directory, allowing for modular development and easier maintenance. The master blueprint file, such as **`api_blueprint.bru`**, aggregates all endpoint definitions and references shared schemas, creating a unified and comprehensive API design. This confirms that any request or response adheres to the defined contracts.

API Design Version Control

As you know, version control is a must for software development. It helps teams manage changes to their code. In the world of API design, version control is even more important. It helps us keep track of changes to things like endpoint definitions, data schemas, and configuration settings. It also lets us see how the API changes over time, which is important for keeping things under control. This is especially important for the Lumina project, where we're constantly adding new features, improvements, and fixes as we go. Plus, version control lets us experiment with changes without messing up the main code. This way, we can review, test, and merge any changes only after we've checked them out, keeping the API design solid.

Version Control with Git

For our Lumina API project, Git is a natural choice for managing version control due to its widespread adoption and powerful feature set. We can leverage Git to track changes in our endpoint blueprints, configuration files, and schema definitions.

Following are some of the essential strategies for integrating Git into our API design process:

Repository Initialization

We begin by initializing a Git repository in our project's root directory. This repository will house all the source files, including our API blueprints written in Bru Lang, configuration files, and supporting documentation.

A typical command to initialize the repository in a Linux environment is:

```
cd lumina-api
git init
```

After initialization, it is important to commit the initial version of our API design files. This commit represents the baseline for all future modifications.

Structured Commit Messages

It is well established that version control depends on clear, descriptive commit messages that document what has changed and why. So here, we establish a convention for commit messages that reflects the changes made to endpoints, data schemas, or configuration settings.

For example:

- **`feat(user): add new fields to user schema`**
- **`fix(auth): resolve validation issues in login endpoint`**
- **`refactor(api): reorganize endpoints for clarity`**

These above messages assist in understanding the evolution of the API design and facilitate easier navigation through the project history.

Branching Strategy

A branching strategy supports concurrent development efforts, ensuring that experimental changes do not interfere with the stable version of our API. For the Lumina project, we may adopt a branching model where:

- **Main Branch (main/master)** contains the stable, production-ready version of the API design.
- **Feature Branches** can be used for developing new endpoints or significant changes. Once reviewed and tested, changes from these branches can be merged back into the main branch.
- **Hotfix Branches** can be dedicated to address critical issues quickly without waiting for the next scheduled update.

Managing Schema Changes and API Versioning

Versioning our API is essential to handle changes without disrupting existing consumers. The version control system can track schema updates, endpoint modifications, and overall API evolution by incorporating version identifiers in the URL, such as **/v1/users** or **/v2/sessions**.

Schema Versioning

Schema changes are managed by creating new versions of the data contracts. For example, if the user schema requires additional fields or modifications to the existing structure, a new version of the schema is defined. The version identifier is then reflected in the API endpoint URL. This strategy allows client applications to choose which version to interact with, ensuring backward compatibility. When a breaking change is necessary, a new branch of the schema is developed, tested, and deployed, while existing versions continue to function for legacy systems.

Tracking Changes with Git

Each change to the schema or endpoint definition is recorded as a commit in Git. Developers can review the differences between commits using Git's diff tools, which clearly show the modifications made in each update. This granular visibility is invaluable for troubleshooting issues that arise from schema modifications or endpoint changes. It also supports auditability, enabling teams to verify that all changes have been properly documented and reviewed.

Sample Program: Version Control Workflow

To illustrate it practically, consider the following workflow for updating the user registration endpoint:

Branch Creation

Create a new branch dedicated to adding an optional field (e.g., **referralCode**) in the user schema:

```
git checkout -b feature/add-referral-code
```

Schema Update

Modify the user schema in the blueprint file to include the new field:

```
// Updated user schema in the registration endpoint
endpoint /users {
  method: POST;
```

```
  request: {
    body: {
      username: string,
      email: string,
      password: string,
      referralCode?: string,  // Optional field for referral
code
      // ... existing fields remain unchanged
    }
  };
  // ... response and error definitions remain unchanged
}
```

Commit Changes

Once the modifications are complete and tested locally, commit the changes with a clear message:

```
 git add api_blueprint.bru
git commit -m "feat(user): add optional referralCode field to
user registration"
```

Code Review and Merge

Open a pull request to merge the changes into the main branch. After review and approval, merge the branch:

```
 git checkout main
git merge feature/add-referral-code
```

Release Tagging

If this update represents a new API version, tag the release accordingly:

```
 git tag v1.1
git push origin main --tags
```

This above program illustrates how version control is used not only to track changes but also to manage the evolution of the API in a controlled, systematic manner. It highlights the practical integration of Git into our development workflow and underscores the benefits of structured version control in maintaining high-quality API designs.

The structured approach to versioning not only facilitates collaboration and continuous integration but also provides a clear path for handling schema evolution and managing endpoint modifications over time.

Documenting Lumina API Specifications

The documentation serves as a reference that aids in understanding how the API functions, what each endpoint requires, and how responses are structured. It also helps team members coordinate effectively, ensuring that updates and new features are implemented consistently. With well-maintained documentation, new contributors can quickly grasp the system's design, and integration with other services becomes more manageable.

Collaborative Documentation Techniques

Using Version-Controlled Documentation Files

One effective approach involves maintaining documentation within version-controlled files alongside the API blueprints. For the Lumina project, the documentation can be stored in Markdown format and organized in a dedicated directory. This method allows every update to be tracked, and it makes it easy to review changes over time. By integrating documentation with Git, the team can use commit messages to explain why certain design decisions were made, and pull requests can include documentation updates to reflect modifications in the API.

For instance, a directory structure might look like this:

```
lumina-api/
├── docs/
│   ├── overview.md
│   ├── endpoints.md
│   ├── schemas.md
│   └── version_history.md
├── endpoints/
│   ├── create_user.bru
│   ├── get_user.bru
│   ├── update_user.bru
```

```
│   └── delete_user.bru
└── schemas/
    └── user.schema.bru
```

This structure ensures that every aspect of the API is documented and kept up-to-date with the actual codebase.

Integrating Documentation Tools

Another practical method is to integrate documentation tools that can generate interactive API documentation automatically from our specifications. Tools such as Swagger or Postman's documentation generator can be adapted for use with our Bruno blueprints. These tools parse the API definitions and create a visual representation of endpoints, request formats, and response structures. Although Bruno's environment is central to our work, leveraging these external tools can provide a user-friendly interface that enhances collaboration and serves as a reference point for external stakeholders.

Using such tools, a continuous integration pipeline might automatically update documentation whenever changes are pushed to the repository. This automation reduces manual effort and ensures that documentation reflects the latest API state.

Implementing Documentation in Bruno

In Bruno, you can reference external docs in config files, and developers can include comments in their Bru Lang scripts that'll be automatically extracted to generate API references that are easy for people to understand. If you embed comments and annotations in the code, the docs will stay closely tied to the API definitions, reducing the risk of discrepancies between the code and its documentation.

For example, a comment block in a Bru Lang file might look like this:

```
// Endpoint: User Registration

// Description: Registers a new user by accepting the required fields and optional profile details.

// Request Body:

//   - username: string (unique identifier)

//   - email: string (must be a valid email)

//   - password: string (min 8 characters)

//   - profile: object (includes firstName, lastName, address, and contacts)
```

```
// Response:
//    - id: number (auto-generated unique user ID)
//    - createdAt: datetime (timestamp of registration)
// Errors:
//    - 400: InvalidInput - Missing or invalid data.
//    - 409: UserExists - Username or email already in use.
endpoint /users {
  method: POST;
  request: { /* ... */ };
  response: { /* ... */ };
  error: { /* ... */ };
}
```

These annotations provide immediate context to anyone reading the code, and tools can parse these comments to build dynamic documentation pages. The techniques outlined above establish a structured process for documenting the Lumina API specifications.

Summary

Here's what we've learned: we nailed a detailed framework for designing the Lumina API project by clearly defining its specs and setting up a solid foundation for future development. We started by detailing both functional and non-functional requirements, which made sure that every aspect of the API—from user management to session handling—was planned out. We outlined specific actions like user registration, data retrieval, updates, and deletions while incorporating precise performance benchmarks and security protocols. We also created these detailed data contracts, where each field in the user schema was defined with clear data types, constraints, and descriptions to avoid any confusion.

We documented how clients and the API interact with each other, explaining how requests and responses should be structured in different scenarios, including error handling. And finally, we integrated all these specifications into the Bruno environment, so that we could automatically validate everything and make sure that every update stayed true to the original design.

CHAPTER 4: BUILDING API WITH BRU LANG

Overview

In this chapter, we will build a practical API using Bru Lang, transitioning from our design phase to concrete implementation. We will begin by configuring an efficient coding environment tailored for our Lumina project, ensuring that all necessary tools and settings are in place for seamless development.

Next, we will implement the core endpoints that form the backbone of our API, including user registration, retrieval, update, and deletion. As we progress, we will embed business logic directly into these endpoints to handle real-world operations such as data validation, password hashing, and timestamp management. Additionally, we will learn how to manage data transformations—normalizing, converting, and enriching data—to maintain consistency throughout the API. Robust error handling techniques will also be introduced to catch and manage issues like invalid input, type mismatches, and transformation failures, ensuring that clear and actionable feedback is provided when errors occur.

By the end of this chapter, we will have developed a dynamic, fully functional API that not only processes data accurately but also adapts to the practical demands of real-world usage, setting the stage for future enhancements and integrations.

Configuring API Coding Environment

Although Bruno is installed and we have already put it into use, our project requires a complete setup that includes a reliable IDE, proper environment variables, and integrated testing tools.

Setting up IDE and Editor

For our live learning, we will choose Visual Studio Code (VS Code) as our IDE, since it offers a user-friendly interface with features like syntax highlighting, integrated terminal access, and Git support, making it an excellent choice for our API development. Apart from this, I personally recommend to install some of the following extensions too:

- **JSON Tool** for formatting and validating our configuration files.
- **GitLens** to improve Git integration and facilitate version control operations.
- **Bracket Pair Colorizer** to visually distinguish code blocks in Bru Lang files.
- **Markdown All in One** to help with collaborative documentation.

Once done with installing all of the above and the VS Code, create a dedicated workspace for the Lumina project. Open the project folder in VS Code, and adjust the workspace settings to automatically format code on save.

Configuring Environment Variables

To streamline our development, we define environment variables that will be used across our project. These variables ensure that our scripts and commands reference consistent paths and settings.

So in our sample program, add the following lines to your shell configuration file (e.g., **.bashrc** or **.zshrc**):

```
export LUMINA_API_PATH="$HOME/lumina-api"

export BRUNO_CONFIG_PATH="$HOME/.bruno/config.json"
```

Next, reload your shell configuration to apply the changes immediately. These variables will simplify our commands by eliminating hard-coded paths and make it easier to share the setup with fellow learners.

Creating the Project Directory and Version Control

Once the environment variables are configured, create a dedicated project directory for Lumina:

```
mkdir -p "$LUMINA_API_PATH"

cd "$LUMINA_API_PATH"
```

Then, you need to initialize a Git repository in this directory to manage the project version control by running the following command:

```
git init
```

After initialization, create a basic **.gitignore** file to prevent unnecessary files from being committed as below:

```
node_modules/

*.log

*.tmp

.vscode/
```

This confirms that the temporary files and local configuration settings are not tracked, which ultimately helps our repository clean, and thereby focused on our core API design.

Integrating Testing Tools

It's really important to have testing tools in place to support our live learning experience. We'll be using a simple testing framework that you can run from the command line. For example, you can use a Node.js-based testing library like Mocha to run tests that simulate API requests.

Alternatively, you can write basic shell scripts to test your endpoints using **curl**. For our example, we will use a shell script that tests the user registration endpoint:

```
#!/bin/bash
# Test the user registration endpoint
response=$(curl -s -X POST http://localhost:3000/users \
  -H "Content-Type: application/json" \
  -d '{
    "username": "testuser",
    "email": "test@gitforgits.com",
    "password": "SecurePass123",
    "profile": {
      "firstName": "Test",
      "lastName": "User",
      "address": {
        "street": "123 Main St",
        "city": "Sample City",
        "postalCode": "12345",
        "country": "ExampleLand"
      },
      "contacts": [{
        "type": "mobile",
        "number": "1234567890"
      }]
    },
    "settings": {
      "preferences": ["news", "updates"],
      "notifications": true
    }
  }')
```

```
echo "Response from registration endpoint: $response"
```

Save this script as **test_registration.sh** in your project directory and make it executable:

```
chmod +x test_registration.sh
```

Once you run this script, it will simulate a user registration request, and you can verify that the endpoint responds as expected.

Automating Setup Process

To make the environment setup reproducible and easy for every learner, we can create an automated setup script. This script will install dependencies, set environment variables, and initialize the project directory along with version control.

```
#!/bin/bash

# Install necessary packages (if not already installed)

# For demonstration purposes, we assume that Git, Node.js, and
npm are pre-installed

# Set up environment variables

echo 'export LUMINA_API_PATH="$HOME/lumina-api"' >> ~/.bashrc

echo 'export BRUNO_CONFIG_PATH="$HOME/.bruno/config.json"' >>
~/.bashrc

source ~/.bashrc

# Create project directory

mkdir -p "$LUMINA_API_PATH"

cd "$LUMINA_API_PATH"

# Initialize Git repository if it doesn't exist

if [ ! -d ".git" ]; then

    git init

    echo "Initialized empty Git repository in
$LUMINA_API_PATH"

fi

echo "Development environment setup is complete."
```

Run the script using:

```
./setup.sh
```

This script will ensure that everyone following along sets up an identical environment, which is critical for a live learning experience. Now you must save the script as **`setup.sh`** in your home directory or project directory in order to have this automation in place in future.

Following these steps let us set up a coding environment that's specifically tailored for Bruno and Bru Lang. This environment ensures that our Lumina API project is supported by an efficient and reproducible setup.

Sample Program: Implementing Core Endpoints

We will now perform live coding of the primary endpoints for the Lumina API using Bru Lang. We will go through the process of writing and understanding the code that forms the backbone of our API, which we learned so far in the previous chapters. We will implement the endpoints for creating, retrieving, updating, and deleting user resources. We will make sure that each endpoint adheres to the specifications and blueprints we have defined earlier.

Creating User Registration Endpoint

We begin with the user registration endpoint, which is responsible for creating new user accounts. This endpoint accepts a POST request with a detailed request payload that includes user details, profile information, and settings. The response confirms the creation by returning a unique user ID and a timestamp.

Below is the live code example for the user registration endpoint:

```
// User Registration Endpoint
endpoint /users {
  method: POST;
  request: {
    body: {
      username: string,        // Unique username, 3-30
characters
      email: string,           // Valid email address
      password: string,        // Secure password, minimum 8
characters
```

```
    profile: {              // Nested profile details
      firstName: string,
      lastName: string,
      address: {
        street: string,
        city: string,
        postalCode: string,
        country: string
      },
      contacts: [
        {
          type: string,       // E.g., mobile, home, work
          number: string
        }
      ],
      socialMedia?: {         // Optional social media handles
        twitter: string?,
        facebook: string?,
        instagram: string?
      }
    },
    settings: {             // User-specific settings
      preferences: [string],
      notifications: boolean
    }
  }
};
response: {
  status: 201;
```

```
    body: {
      id: number,                    // Auto-generated user
identifier
      username: string,
      email: string,
      profile: {
        firstName: string,
        lastName: string,
        address: {
          street: string,
          city: string,
          postalCode: string,
          country: string
        },
        contacts: [
          {
            type: string,
            number: string
          }
        ],
        socialMedia?: {             // Optional social media handles
          twitter: string?,
          facebook: string?,
          instagram: string?
        }
      },
      settings: {
        preferences: [string],
        notifications: boolean
```

```
      },
      createdAt: datetime      // Timestamp of user creation
    }
  };
  error: {
    400: {
      error: "InvalidInput",
      message: "Required fields are missing or contain invalid
data."
    },
    409: {
      error: "UserExists",
      message: "A user with the provided email or username
already exists."
    }
  }
}
```

In the above script, we define the endpoint using Bru Lang syntax. The request body details the necessary fields, including a nested profile object and optional social media data. The response section confirms that on a successful registration, the API returns a status code of 201 along with the user's details.

Retrieving User Details

Next, we implement an endpoint for retrieving user details. This endpoint utilizes a GET request and expects a path parameter (user ID) to identify the user. The response returns the complete user record, mirroring the structure defined during registration.

```
// Retrieve User Details Endpoint
endpoint /users/{id} {
  method: GET;
  request: {
    params: {
```

```
    id: number              // Unique user identifier
  }
};
response: {
  status: 200;
  body: {
    id: number,
    username: string,
    email: string,
    profile: {
      firstName: string,
      lastName: string,
      address: {
        street: string,
        city: string,
        postalCode: string,
        country: string
      },
      contacts: [
        {
          type: string,
          number: string
        }
      ],
      socialMedia?: {       // Optional social media handles
        twitter: string?,
        facebook: string?,
        instagram: string?
      }
```

```
      },
      settings: {
        preferences: [string],
        notifications: boolean
      },
      createdAt: datetime       // Timestamp of account creation
    }
  };
  error: {
    404: {
      error: "NotFound",
      message: "User not found with the given identifier."
    }
  }
}
```

This endpoint confirms that a GET request with a valid user ID returns a comprehensive user record.

Updating User Information

You can update user details using this endpoint, which uses the PUT method. This allows clients to modify one or more fields of an existing user record. The fields are marked optional, so you can update just some of the information without having to resubmit everything.

```
// Update User Information Endpoint
endpoint /users/{id} {
  method: PUT;
  request: {
    params: {
      id: number                // Unique identifier for the user
to be updated
    },
```

```
body: {
  username: string?,      // Optional update of username
  email: string?,         // Optional update of email
  password: string?,      // Optional update of password
  profile: {              // Optional profile updates
    firstName: string?,
    lastName: string?,
    address: {
      street: string?,
      city: string?,
      postalCode: string?,
      country: string?
    },
    contacts: [
      {
        type: string,
        number: string
      }
    ]?,
    socialMedia?: {        // Optional social media updates
      twitter: string?,
      facebook: string?,
      instagram: string?
    }
  }?,
  settings: {             // Optional settings update
    preferences: [string]?,
    notifications: boolean?
  }?
```

```
  }
};
response: {
  status: 200;
  body: {
    id: number,
    username: string,
    email: string,
    profile: {
      firstName: string,
      lastName: string,
      address: {
        street: string,
        city: string,
        postalCode: string,
        country: string
      },
      contacts: [
        {
          type: string,
          number: string
        }
      ],
      socialMedia?: {
        twitter: string?,
        facebook: string?,
        instagram: string?
      }
    },
```

```
      settings: {
        preferences: [string],
        notifications: boolean
      },
      updatedAt: datetime    // Timestamp marking the update
    }
  };
  error: {
    400: {
      error: "InvalidInput",
      message: "Provided data for update is invalid."
    },
    404: {
      error: "NotFound",
      message: "User not found for the given identifier."
    }
  }
}
```

The update endpoint demonstrates flexibility by allowing optional fields, so clients can send only the information they wish to change. The response confirms the successful update and includes an updated timestamp.

Deleting User

Finally, we implement the user deletion endpoint, which uses the DELETE method. This endpoint validates the provided user ID and, upon successful deletion, returns a 204 status code with an empty body to indicate that the resource has been removed.

```
// Delete User Endpoint
endpoint /users/{id} {
  method: DELETE;
  request: {
```

```
    params: {
        id: number                    // Unique identifier for the user
to be deleted
    }
  };
  response: {
    status: 204;                      // No content returned for a
successful deletion
    body: {}                          // Empty response signifies
deletion success
  };
  error: {
    404: {
        error: "NotFound",
        message: "User not found for the provided identifier."
    }
  }
}
```

This endpoint is straightforward and confirms that deletion operations are handled with clear and minimal responses. It will make sure that the clients are immediately aware of the outcome.

To sum up quickly, each of the endpoint was coded in a way that adheres to our previously established specifications and blueprints. This systematic approach not only makes our API consistent and predictable but also provides a clear pathway for future enhancements. In subsequent topics, we will build upon these core endpoints by integrating business logic, managing data transformations, and adding advanced features that further enrich the Lumina API.

Embedding Business Logic into API Endpoints

The concept of business logic refers to the set of rules that govern how data is processed and manipulated within an application. For our Lumina API project, this means that every endpoint will not only validate incoming data but also execute operations such as checking for existing users, hashing passwords, or updating timestamps. The idea is to keep the core endpoint definitions separate from the logic that drives real-world functionality.

Business Logic Techniques

There are multiple techniques to integrate business logic into endpoints, and each has its advantages. We will explore two primary strategies that work well in our context: inline logic within the endpoint definition and external service integration.

Inline Business Logic

Inline business logic involves embedding the rules directly within the endpoint's execution flow. This technique is useful when the logic is simple and closely tied to the specific endpoint. For example, in the user registration endpoint, we might need to check if a username already exists, hash the provided password, and set a creation timestamp.

Following are the steps for Inline Logic:

1. We first verify that the incoming request meets all validation requirements. This can include checking for the presence of required fields, ensuring correct data types, and performing initial sanitization.
2. Next, we incorporate conditions to enforce business rules. For instance, if a user with the same email exists, the logic should trigger an error response before proceeding further.
3. After that, we process the data as needed—for example, hashing a password using a secure algorithm. This transformation occurs before the data is stored or further processed.
4. And finally, once the primary operation is completed, there are some additional steps such as setting timestamps or triggering notifications which can be performed.

Below is a modified version of our user registration endpoint that includes inline business logic using pseudo-code annotations within Bru Lang:

```
endpoint /users {
  method: POST;
  request: {
    body: {
      username: string,
      email: string,
      password: string,
      profile: { /* nested profile details */ },
      settings: { /* user settings */ }
    }
```

```
  };
  // Inline business logic starts here
  logic: {
    // Check if the user already exists in the database
    if (db.exists("users", { email: request.body.email }) ||
        db.exists("users", { username: request.body.username
})) {
      return error(409, {
        error: "UserExists",
        message: "A user with the provided email or username
already exists."
      });
    }

    // Securely hash the password before storage
    let hashedPassword = security.hash(request.body.password);
    request.body.password = hashedPassword;

    // Set creation timestamp
    request.body.createdAt = datetime.now();

    // Save the new user record to the database
    let newUser = db.insert("users", request.body);

    // Optionally trigger a welcome notification (e.g., send
email)
    notifications.send("welcome", newUser.email);

    // Return the created user record
    return response(201, {
```

```
      id: newUser.id,
      username: newUser.username,
      email: newUser.email,
      profile: newUser.profile,
      settings: newUser.settings,
      createdAt: newUser.createdAt
    });
  };
  // Inline business logic ends here
  error: {
    400: {
      error: "InvalidInput",
      message: "Required fields are missing or contain invalid
data."
    }
  }
}
```

In this sample program, the inline logic directly addresses user existence checks, password hashing, timestamp setting, database insertion, and even triggering notifications. The use of inline logic is straightforward and effective when the operations are self-contained within the endpoint.

External Service Integration

For more complex scenarios or when business logic needs to be reused across multiple endpoints, integrating external services or microservices can be more beneficial. This approach separates the business logic from the API layer, enabling better modularity and reuse.

Following are the steps for External Service Integration:

1. At first, we identify common business operations that can be abstracted into separate services. For instance, authentication, user verification, and notification handling might be implemented as standalone services.
2. Next, we use an API gateway or a middleware layer that delegates requests to the appropriate service. This layer acts as a coordinator, ensuring that each endpoint calls the necessary services to complete the business operations.

3. We then implement inter-service communication using REST, gRPC, or message queues. This decouples the core API endpoints from the business logic, facilitating easier updates and scaling.
4. And finally, we ensure that the system gracefully handles failures in external services by implementing fallback logic.

So let us assume that our Lumina API offloads user validation and password hashing to an external authentication service. The endpoint would then be simplified as follows:

```
endpoint /users {
  method: POST;
  request: {
    body: {
      username: string,
      email: string,
      password: string,
      profile: { /* nested profile details */ },
      settings: { /* user settings */ }
    }
  };
  logic: {
    // Delegate business logic to an external authentication
service
    let result =
externalService.call("authService.createUser", request.body);

    // Check if the external service returned an error
    if (result.error) {
      return error(result.errorCode, result.errorDetails);
    }

    // Return the response from the external service
    return response(201, result.data);
```

```
  };
  error: {
    400: {
      error: "InvalidInput",
      message: "Required fields are missing or contain invalid
data."
    }
  }
}
```

In this method, the endpoint defers the heavy lifting to the **`authService.createUser`** method, making the API endpoint code cleaner and more focused on routing. This method works well in larger projects where business logic is complex and shared across multiple endpoints.

Strategy Selection Guidance

Now when choosing between inline business logic and external service integration, you need to think or try considering the following factors:

- If the business logic is straightforward and unique to the endpoint, inline logic is often more efficient. For shared, complex logic that may be reused or require independent scaling, external service integration is preferable.
- Inline logic is simpler to implement and understand for small-scale projects. However, as the project grows, separating business logic into external services can help reduce code duplication and improve overall maintainability.
- External services allow for independent scaling of business logic. This can be advantageous if certain operations, such as authentication, require more resources during peak usage periods.

Managing Data Transformations and Error Handling

So, as data moves from one place to another—like from incoming requests to our business logic and then to the responses sent back to clients—it often needs to be converted, normalized, or enriched to meet the API's requirements.It's also important to be ready for, detect, and manage any potential errors that might pop up during these transformations.Basically, our goal is to come up with strategies that keep data integrity and consistency while also providing clear, actionable feedback when issues arise.

Data Transformations Techniques

Data transformation involves converting data from one format or structure into another. In the context of our Lumina API, data transformations may include:

- Converting data types, such as transforming string representations of dates into a standardized datetime format or converting numeric strings into integers or floats. For example, ensuring that a timestamp sent as a string is converted to a proper datetime object before storage or further processing.
- Adjusting the data to a consistent format. This could involve trimming whitespace, converting text to a standard case (e.g., lower-case for emails), or formatting phone numbers uniformly.
- Adding derived values or computed properties. For instance, when creating a user, we might compute an initial user score based on default preferences or derive a full name from first and last names.
- Checking data for correctness and removing any unwanted or potentially harmful content. This is critical for preventing issues like SQL injection or other forms of data corruption.

So let us say that when a new user registers, the incoming data may require a few transformations before being processed:

1. Convert the email address to lower-case to ensure consistency.
2. Transform the provided date string (if any) into a standardized datetime object.
3. Though not strictly a transformation, ensuring the password is processed (hashed) is part of preparing the data for secure storage.

I am providing you a sample inline transformation block within the endpoint logic, which might look like this:

```
logic: {
  // Normalize email to lower-case
  request.body.email = request.body.email.toLowerCase();
  // Convert any date string to a datetime object (if
applicable)
  // Example: Convert a 'dob' field if provided
  if (request.body.dob) {
    request.body.dob = datetime.parse(request.body.dob);
```

```
    }
    // Hash the password for secure storage
    request.body.password =
security.hash(request.body.password);
    // Continue with business logic...
}
```

This code ensures that the data we process is consistent and safe for further operations.

Coping with Error Handling

Errors happen, and it's important to handle them well. When we do that, our API can deal with issues, give useful feedback to clients, and keep the system stable. Errors can pop up in different places, like during data changes, when business logic is running, or when we're interacting with outside services.

Common Errors

While developing the Lumina API, we anticipated several types of errors that might arise:

1. If incoming data does not conform to the expected format (e.g., an improperly formatted date or email), transformation functions may fail.
2. Required fields might be absent from the request, leading to incomplete data processing.
3. Data may be of an unexpected type (e.g., a string provided where a number is expected), causing conversion functions to error out.
4. Functions that parse or convert data (like date parsing) might throw exceptions if the input is invalid.
5. If data transformations rely on external libraries or services (for example, a third-party validation service), those dependencies may fail or return errors.

Robust Error Handling Methods

To handle these potential errors, we implement several strategies:

- Before performing transformations, validate that the incoming data meets the basic requirements. Use built-in validation functions to check for required fields and correct data types.
- Enclose transformation code in error-handling constructs to catch exceptions and prevent system crashes. In our pseudo-code, we simulate this by checking for error conditions and returning structured error responses.

- Log errors with detailed information about the context and data that caused the error. This practice aids in debugging and improving the system over time.
- Ensure that error responses are clear and actionable. Clients should receive not only an error code but also a message that explains what went wrong and, if possible, how to correct it.

Sample Program: Error Handling during Data Transformation

We will enhance our user registration endpoint with robust error handling that covers common transformation errors. Suppose we want to handle the situation where the date of birth is not in a valid format. So here, we can implement a check and return a structured error message if the parsing fails.

```
endpoint /users {
  method: POST;
  request: {
    body: {
      username: string,
      email: string,
      password: string,
      dob?: string,               // Optional date of birth as a
string
      profile: { /* nested profile details */ },
      settings: { /* user settings */ }
    }
  };
  logic: {
    // Normalize email to lower-case
    request.body.email = request.body.email.toLowerCase();
    // Attempt to parse 'dob' if provided
    if (request.body.dob) {
      let parsedDob = datetime.parse(request.body.dob);
      if (!parsedDob) {
        return error(400, {
```

```
        error: "InvalidDateFormat",
        message: "The date of birth provided is not in a
valid format. Please use YYYY-MM-DD."
      });
    }
    request.body.dob = parsedDob;
  }
  // Hash the password securely
  request.body.password =
security.hash(request.body.password);
  // Proceed with business logic: check for existing user,
insert new user record, etc.
  if (db.exists("users", { email: request.body.email })) {
    return error(409, {
      error: "UserExists",
      message: "A user with the provided email already
exists."
    });
  }
  request.body.createdAt = datetime.now();
  let newUser = db.insert("users", request.body);
  // Return the newly created user data
  return response(201, {
    id: newUser.id,
    username: newUser.username,
    email: newUser.email,
    profile: newUser.profile,
    settings: newUser.settings,
    createdAt: newUser.createdAt
  });
```

```
  };
  error: {
    400: {
      error: "InvalidInput",
      message: "Required fields are missing or contain invalid
data."
    }
  }
}
```

In this enhanced endpoint, we explicitly check if the optional **dob** field is provided. The **datetime.parse()** function attempts to convert the string into a datetime object. If the parsing fails (i.e., the function returns a falsy value), we immediately return a 400 error with a clear message about the expected date format.

Other errors might occur during transformations. For instance, if a numeric field unexpectedly receives non-numeric input, similar validation and error-handling steps should be applied. Although our example focuses on date parsing, the same principles apply across all data types.

Summary

To sum it up, we learned how to build our API using Bru Lang in a live coding environment. We set up our coding setup by creating a complete development workspace with an IDE, environment variables, and integrated testing tools, so that anyone could easily set up the same thing. We then created core endpoints for operations such as user registration, retrieval, update, and deletion, turning our API blueprints into practical, executable code.

We put business logic directly into the endpoints to handle essential operations like validating input data, hashing passwords, and managing timestamps. This brought real-world functionality to our Lumina project. We also addressed data transformations by normalizing inputs, converting data types, and enriching information. We also set up solid error-handling mechanisms to catch common problems like invalid data formats, missing fields, and type mismatches, giving clients clear, actionable error responses. In short, the chapter showed a practical and integrated way to build and improve API endpoints with business logic, data changes, and error handling.

CHAPTER 5: TESTING API FUNCTIONALITIES

Overview

In this chapter, we will explore how to rigorously test the Lumina API to ensure that every endpoint meets its functional requirements and behaves reliably under various conditions. We will begin by developing automated test suites that simulate real user interactions, such as creating, retrieving, updating, and deleting user data. Following this, we will conduct end-to-end testing to validate the entire workflow of our API, confirming that it responds correctly from the moment a request is sent until a complete response is received.

We will then simulate diverse operational scenarios—ranging from high concurrency and network latency to malformed requests and unauthorized access—to observe how our API handles stress and errors. Finally, we will learn to assess the test results, spot any issues or bugs, and apply practical debugging techniques to resolve them. By the end of this chapter, we will have a robust testing framework in place that validates the functionality and stability of our API, and also serves as a foundation for continuous integration and future enhancements.

Developing Automated Test Suites

An automated test suite is basically a set of tests that run automatically to make sure our endpoints are working right. They cover all sorts of scenarios, from regular use cases to edge cases that might cause errors.

The main goals are:

- Verifying that the API endpoints return the correct status codes and data structures.
- Ensuring that data transformations and business logic are applied correctly.
- Validating that error responses are triggered for invalid input or operational failures.
- Providing a safety net that supports continuous integration and continuous deployment (CI/CD).

These automated tests save time, reduce manual testing errors, and offer a consistent way to validate changes as the API evolves.

Testing Tools and Frameworks

For our live learning experience, we will use a combination of shell scripts with **`curl`** commands and Node.js-based testing frameworks. This dual approach offers both simplicity and the power of automated assertions. Specifically, we can:

- Use **`curl`** to simulate HTTP requests directly from the command line.
- Leverage **Mocha** or **Jest** for more complex test scenarios in Node.js if needed.
- Integrate test scripts into a CI/CD pipeline so that tests run automatically on every

commit.

For this chapter, we will start with basic shell scripts to illustrate the principles and then outline how to extend these tests using a Node.js framework.

Creating Basic Test Suite

Testing User Registration Endpoint

A basic test for our user registration endpoint can be created using a shell script. The script sends a POST request with a sample payload and then verifies the HTTP status code and parts of the response.

Given below is a sample test script:

```
#!/bin/bash
# Define the API endpoint and sample payload
API_URL="http://localhost:3000/users"
PAYLOAD='{
  "username": "testuser",
  "email": "test@gitforgits.com",
  "password": "SecurePass123",
  "profile": {
    "firstName": "Test",
    "lastName": "User",
    "address": {
      "street": "123 Main St",
      "city": "Sample City",
      "postalCode": "12345",
      "country": "ExampleLand"
    },
    "contacts": [
      {"type": "mobile", "number": "1234567890"}
    ]
  },
```

```
  "settings": {
    "preferences": ["news", "updates"],
    "notifications": true
  }
}'
# Send the POST request
response=$(curl -s -w "\n%{http_code}" -X POST $API_URL -H
"Content-Type: application/json" -d "$PAYLOAD")
# Split the response and status code
http_body=$(echo "$response" | sed '$d')
http_code=$(echo "$response" | tail -n1)
# Check if the status code is 201 for a successful
registration
if [ "$http_code" -eq 201 ]; then
  echo "User registration test passed. Status code:
$http_code"
else
  echo "User registration test failed. Status code:
$http_code"
  echo "Response body: $http_body"
fi
```

This script defines the endpoint URL, constructs a sample JSON payload, and uses **`curl`** to send a POST request. It then checks if the HTTP status code is 201 (indicating success) and outputs a message accordingly.

Testing User Retrieval Endpoint

Similarly, we can create a test for retrieving user details. This test assumes that a user with a known identifier exists.

See the following script:

```
#!/bin/bash
# Define the API endpoint for retrieving user details
```

```
USER_ID=1
API_URL="http://localhost:3000/users/$USER_ID"
# Send the GET request
response=$(curl -s -w "\n%{http_code}" -X GET $API_URL -H
"Content-Type: application/json")
http_body=$(echo "$response" | sed '$d')
http_code=$(echo "$response" | tail -n1)
# Check if the status code is 200
if [ "$http_code" -eq 200 ]; then
  echo "User retrieval test passed. Status code: $http_code"
else
  echo "User retrieval test failed. Status code: $http_code"
  echo "Response body: $http_body"
fi
```

This test sends a GET request to fetch a user's details by user ID and validates that the returned status code is 200.

Using Mocha

For more complex test scenarios, a Node.js framework like Mocha can be used to write tests with richer assertions. I have outline a simplified example using Mocha and Chai:

First, initialize the Node.js project in the Lumina API directory:

```
npm init -y
npm install mocha chai axios --save-dev
```

Then, create a test file (e.g., `test/api.test.js`):

```
const axios = require('axios');
const chai = require('chai');
const expect = chai.expect;
const API_URL = "http://localhost:3000/users";
describe("Lumina API Tests", function() {
```

```
  it("should register a new user", async function() {
    const payload = {
      username: "testuser2",
      email: "test2@gitforgits.com",
      password: "SecurePass123",
      profile: {
        firstName: "Test",
        lastName: "User",
        address: {
          street: "456 Main St",
          city: "Sample City",
          postalCode: "12345",
          country: "ExampleLand"
        },
        contacts: [{ type: "mobile", number: "0987654321" }]
      },
      settings: {
        preferences: ["news", "updates"],
        notifications: true
      }
    };
    const response = await axios.post(API_URL, payload);
    expect(response.status).to.equal(201);
    expect(response.data).to.have.property("id");
  });
  it("should retrieve user details", async function() {
    const userId = 1; // Replace with a valid user ID for
testing
    const response = await axios.get(`${API_URL}/${userId}`);
```

```
    expect(response.status).to.equal(200);
    expect(response.data).to.have.property("username");
    expect(response.data).to.have.property("email");
  });
});
```

Add a test script to your **package.json**:

```
"scripts": {
  "test": "mocha"
}
```

Execute the tests:

```
npm test
```

With this Node.js test suite, we use Axios for HTTP requests and Chai for assertions, which lets us check the API's responses and data integrity more closely.

Handling Errors in Test Suites

As part of our test suites, we also simulate scenarios where errors are expected. This is essential to confirm that our error handling is robust and provides clear, actionable responses. So here, to test the error response for invalid input, let us create a test case where required fields are missing or contain invalid data:

```
it("should return an error for invalid user registration",
async function() {
  const invalidPayload = {
    username: "tu", // Too short
    email: "not-an-email",
    // password is missing
    profile: {
      firstName: "Test",
      lastName: "User",
      address: {
```

```
      street: "789 Main St",
      city: "Sample City",
      postalCode: "12345",
      country: "ExampleLand"
    },
    contacts: [{ type: "mobile", number: "1234567890" }]
  },
  settings: {
    preferences: ["news", "updates"],
    notifications: true
  }
};
try {
  await axios.post(API_URL, invalidPayload);
} catch (error) {
  expect(error.response.status).to.equal(400);
  expect(error.response.data).to.have.property("error");
}
});
```

This test verifies that when invalid data is submitted, the API returns a 400 status code along with an appropriate error message.

Integrating Automated Tests into Workflow

The integration of these automated test suites into our development workflow ensures that every new code change is verified against our functional requirements. So for this, we setup a CI/CD pipeline to run these tests on every commit, by which we can catch issues early and maintain a high standard of quality. There are tools like GitHub Actions, Jenkins, or GitLab CI which can be configured to run the test suites automatically.

For example, a simple GitHub Actions workflow file (**.github/workflows/test.yml**) might look like this:

```
name: API Test Suite
```

```yaml
on: [push, pull_request]
jobs:
  build:
    runs-on: ubuntu-latest
    steps:
      - name: Checkout code
        uses: actions/checkout@v2

      - name: Set up Node.js
        uses: actions/setup-node@v2
        with:
          node-version: '14'

      - name: Install dependencies
        run: npm install

      - name: Run tests
        run: npm test
```

This configuration ensures that every push or pull request triggers the automated test suite, providing immediate feedback on the health of the API.

This whole approach to testing not only reinforces our API's integrity but also provides a scalable, automated way to validate every future modification such that the Lumina project remains robust and aligned with its functional objectives.

End to End API Testing

When you test from start to finish, you make sure that the whole API works right as one system, from start to finish. This kind of testing makes sure that everything works the way it should by checking:

- The correctness of HTTP status codes.
- The structure and content of the response payloads.

- The proper functioning of business logic, including data transformations and error handling.
- The overall integration of multiple endpoints working together seamlessly.

Using Installed Tools

Our testing strategy will revolve around using **curl** for making HTTP requests and shell scripts to automate these tests. We will also utilize basic command-line text processing utilities (such as **grep**, **sed**, and **awk**) to extract and verify parts of the response. This approach ensures that we remain within the scope of our pre-installed environment.

The testing process will cover the following steps:

1. Use **curl** to simulate client requests (GET, POST, PUT, DELETE) to our API endpoints.
2. Check the HTTP status codes and parse the response bodies to verify that they match the expected format and content.
3. Deliberately trigger error conditions to ensure that our API returns the correct error messages and status codes.

You ha ve to putl all these steps together into shell scripts that can run multiple tests one after the other, giving you a full view of how the API is acting.

Sample Program: End-to-End Testing

Testing User Registration

We begin by testing the user registration endpoint to confirm that a new user can be created successfully. Below is an example shell script that sends a POST request to the **/users** endpoint and checks the response.

```
#!/bin/bash
# Define the endpoint URL and sample payload for registration
API_URL="http://localhost:3000/users"
PAYLOAD='{
  "username": "end2enduser",
  "email": "end2end@gitforgits.com",
  "password": "End2EndPass123",
  "profile": {
```

```
    "firstName": "End",
    "lastName": "User",
    "address": {
      "street": "100 Test Blvd",
      "city": "Testville",
      "postalCode": "98765",
      "country": "Testland"
    },
    "contacts": [
      {"type": "mobile", "number": "5551234567"}
    ]
  },
  "settings": {
    "preferences": ["updates", "alerts"],
    "notifications": true
  }
}'
# Send the POST request and capture the response and status
code
response=$(curl -s -w "\n%{http_code}" -X POST $API_URL -H
"Content-Type: application/json" -d "$PAYLOAD")
http_body=$(echo "$response" | sed '$d')
http_code=$(echo "$response" | tail -n1)
# Validate the response status code and extract the user ID
from the response
if [ "$http_code" -eq 201 ]; then
  user_id=$(echo "$http_body" | grep -o '"id":[^,]*' | awk -F:
'{print $2}' | tr -d ' ')
  echo "User registration test passed. Status code:
$http_code, User ID: $user_id"
else
```

```
  echo "User registration test failed. Status code:
$http_code"
  echo "Response body: $http_body"
fi
```

This script sends a POST request to the user registration endpoint with a sample payload, captures the response, and checks that the HTTP status code is 201. It then extracts the user ID from the response, confirming that the user was created successfully.

Testing User Retrieval

Next, we test the retrieval of user details. This script uses a GET request to fetch the user data using the user ID obtained from the registration test.

```
#!/bin/bash
# Assume USER_ID is obtained from previous registration test
USER_ID=1  # Replace with the actual user ID if known
API_URL="http://localhost:3000/users/$USER_ID"
# Send the GET request to retrieve user details
response=$(curl -s -w "\n%{http_code}" -X GET $API_URL -H
"Content-Type: application/json")
http_body=$(echo "$response" | sed '$d')
http_code=$(echo "$response" | tail -n1)
# Validate the response status code and check for essential
fields
if [ "$http_code" -eq 200 ]; then
  username=$(echo "$http_body" | grep -o '"username":"[^"]*' |
awk -F: '{print $2}' | tr -d '"')
  echo "User retrieval test passed. Status code: $http_code,
Username: $username"
else
  echo "User retrieval test failed. Status code: $http_code"
  echo "Response body: $http_body"
fi
```

This script sends a GET request to the **/users/{id}** endpoint and validates that the response status code is 200. It extracts the username from the response to confirm that the data is returned correctly.

Testing Error Conditions

We also need to confirm that our API handles error conditions appropriately. The following script tests the registration endpoint with an invalid payload—specifically, with a missing password—to ensure that our API returns an appropriate error message.

```
#!/bin/bash
# Define the endpoint URL and an invalid payload (missing password)
API_URL="http://localhost:3000/users"
INVALID_PAYLOAD='{
  "username": "baduser",
  "email": "bad@gitforgits.com",
  "profile": {
    "firstName": "Bad",
    "lastName": "User",
    "address": {
      "street": "200 Fail Rd",
      "city": "Errorville",
      "postalCode": "00000",
      "country": "Nowhere"
    },
    "contacts": [
      {"type": "mobile", "number": "0000000000"}
    ]
  },
  "settings": {
    "preferences": ["none"],
    "notifications": false
```

```
  }
}'
# Send the POST request with the invalid payload
response=$(curl -s -w "\n%{http_code}" -X POST $API_URL -H
"Content-Type: application/json" -d "$INVALID_PAYLOAD")
http_body=$(echo "$response" | sed '$d')
http_code=$(echo "$response" | tail -n1)
# Validate that the API returns a 400 error for invalid input
if [ "$http_code" -eq 400 ]; then
  echo "Invalid registration test passed. Status code:
$http_code"
  echo "Error message: $(echo "$http_body" | grep -o
'"message":"[^"]*' | awk -F: '{print $2}' | tr -d '"')"
else
  echo "Invalid registration test failed. Status code:
$http_code"
  echo "Response body: $http_body"
fi
```

This script intentionally omits the password field in the payload, which is required by our user registration schema. The API should return a 400 status code with an error message indicating the missing or invalid input. The script checks for this condition and prints the error message to confirm that the error handling is working as expected.

Integrating Tests into Workflow

After creating individual test scripts for each endpoint, we can combine them into a comprehensive test suite that runs all tests sequentially. This below master script will execute each test and summarize the outcomes to verify the entire API's functionality in one go.

```
#!/bin/bash
echo "Starting end-to-end API tests for Lumina..."
# Run user registration test
./test_user_registration.sh
```

```
# Capture the registered user ID from the output of the
registration test
# For demonstration, we assume that the USER_ID is stored in a
temporary file
USER_ID=$(cat user_id.txt)
if [ -z "$USER_ID" ]; then
  echo "User registration test failed. Cannot proceed with
further tests."
  exit 1
fi
# Run user retrieval test using the registered user ID
./test_user_retrieval.sh
# Run invalid registration test to check error handling
./test_invalid_registration.sh
echo "End-to-end API tests completed."
```

This master script orchestrates the execution of multiple test scripts. It first runs the user registration test, retrieves the user ID, and then uses that ID to test the retrieval endpoint. It finally runs an invalid registration test to ensure error handling is correctly implemented.

Simulating API Interactions

Let's dive into this module where we'll be testing the Lumina API's strength and flexibility by simulating different user interactions and network scenarios. Our aim is to make sure the API can handle everything from regular use cases to edge cases and even those rare occasions when things might go a bit haywire. We'll be recreating various user behaviors and network situations to make sure our API stays cool, calm, and collected under pressure.

Identifying Potential Disruptive Conditions

Before we start simulating interactions, it is important to outline the various conditions that could impact the API. These include:

- Simulating multiple users making requests simultaneously to test the API's ability to handle load and prevent race conditions.
- Introducing artificial delays to mimic slow network conditions. This tests whether the API handles delayed requests gracefully and returns appropriate timeout errors.

- Sending requests with missing or invalid data to verify that the API's validation and error handling respond appropriately.
- Attempting to access endpoints without proper authentication or authorization to ensure that security measures are enforced.
- Mimicking a user who sends a burst of requests in quick succession, to see if the API can throttle or rate-limit requests to prevent overload.
- Testing how the API reacts when unexpected data types or structures are sent, ensuring that data transformation and validation logic catch these issues.

If we plan for these scenarios, we can design tests that simulate both typical and adverse interactions, making our API more robust.

Simulating High Concurrency

One effective way to simulate high concurrency is by using shell scripting to launch multiple parallel requests. The following script uses a loop to simulate 50 concurrent user registrations. You can adjust the number as needed to stress-test the API.

```
#!/bin/bash
API_URL="http://localhost:3000/users"
# Define the payload template for registration
payload_template='{
  "username": "user%d",
  "email": "user%d@gitforgits.com",
  "password": "SecurePass123",
  "profile": {
    "firstName": "User",
    "lastName": "Test",
    "address": {
      "street": "123 Test St",
      "city": "Testville",
      "postalCode": "12345",
      "country": "Testland"
    },
    "contacts": [
```

```
      {"type": "mobile", "number": "1234567890"}
    ]
  },
  "settings": {
    "preferences": ["news", "updates"],
    "notifications": true
  }
}'
# Function to simulate a registration request
simulate_registration() {
  user_number=$1
  payload=$(printf "$payload_template" "$user_number"
"$user_number")
  response=$(curl -s -w "\n%{http_code}" -X POST "$API_URL" -H
"Content-Type: application/json" -d "$payload")
  http_code=$(echo "$response" | tail -n1)
  echo "User $user_number registration response code:
$http_code"
}
# Launch concurrent requests using a loop
for i in {1..50}; do
  simulate_registration $i &
done
wait
echo "High concurrency simulation completed."
```

This script generates 50 user registrations concurrently, printing out the HTTP status code for each request.

Simulating Network Latency and Timeouts

Now here, to simulate network latency, we can introduce delays in our requests. One way to do this is by using the **sleep** command in a loop. Although we cannot directly control network conditions with **curl**, we can mimic slow client behavior.

Try the following example:

```
#!/bin/bash
API_URL="http://localhost:3000/users"
payload='{
  "username": "latencyuser",
  "email": "latency@gitforgits.com",
  "password": "SecurePass123",
  "profile": {
    "firstName": "Latency",
    "lastName": "Test",
    "address": {
      "street": "456 Delay Ave",
      "city": "Slowtown",
      "postalCode": "54321",
      "country": "Testland"
    },
    "contacts": [
      {"type": "mobile", "number": "0987654321"}
    ]
  },
  "settings": {
    "preferences": ["updates"],
    "notifications": false
  }
}'
echo "Simulating network latency with 5-second delay before sending the request."
sleep 5  # Delay added to simulate latency
```

```
response=$(curl -s -w "\n%{http_code}" -X POST "$API_URL" -H
"Content-Type: application/json" -d "$payload")
http_code=$(echo "$response" | tail -n1)
echo "Response code after delay: $http_code"
```

This script introduces a 5-second delay before sending the registration request.

Simulating Malformed/Incomplete Requests

To make sure everything's working right, it's important to test how the API handles malformed requests. The following script simulates a registration request with missing required fields:

```
#!/bin/bash
API_URL="http://localhost:3000/users"
# Define an invalid payload missing the password field
INVALID_PAYLOAD='{
  "username": "malformeduser",
  "email": "malformed@gitforgits.com",
  "profile": {
    "firstName": "Malformed",
    "lastName": "User",
    "address": {
      "street": "789 Error Rd",
      "city": "Bugsville",
      "postalCode": "00000",
      "country": "Testland"
    },
    "contacts": [
      {"type": "mobile", "number": "0000000000"}
    ]
  },
  "settings": {
```

```
    "preferences": ["none"],
    "notifications": false
  }
}'
response=$(curl -s -w "\n%{http_code}" -X POST "$API_URL" -H
"Content-Type: application/json" -d "$INVALID_PAYLOAD")
http_body=$(echo "$response" | sed '$d')
http_code=$(echo "$response" | tail -n1)
if [ "$http_code" -eq 400 ]; then
  echo "Malformed request test passed. Status code:
$http_code"
  echo "Error details: $(echo "$http_body" | grep -o
'"message":"[^"]*' | awk -F: '{print $2}' | tr -d '"')"
else
  echo "Malformed request test failed. Status code:
$http_code"
  echo "Response body: $http_body"
fi
```

Here, the payload intentionally omits the password field, which is required for user registration. The expected outcome is a 400 error response with a clear error message, verifying that our validation logic catches incomplete data.

Simulating Unauthorized Access

When we test for unauthorized access, we make sure that our API security measures are working right. If the API uses tokens or other forms of authentication, we can simulate unauthorized requests by omitting these credentials.

Here's an example to show you what I mean:

```
#!/bin/bash
# Assume that the /users endpoint requires an authentication
token for updates
USER_ID=1
API_URL="http://localhost:3000/users/$USER_ID"
```

```
# Simulate a PUT request without authentication headers
payload='{
  "username": "unauthorizeduser"
}'
response=$(curl -s -w "\n%{http_code}" -X PUT "$API_URL" -H
"Content-Type: application/json" -d "$payload")
http_code=$(echo "$response" | tail -n1)
if [ "$http_code" -eq 401 ]; then
  echo "Unauthorized access test passed. Status code:
$http_code"
else
  echo "Unauthorized access test failed. Status code:
$http_code"
fi
```

This script sends an update request without the required authentication token, expecting a 401 Unauthorized error. This confirms that our API correctly enforces access controls.

Simulating Rapid Sequential Requests

Now here, to simulate a scenario where a user sends a burst of requests, we can use a loop that sends requests in rapid succession. This test helps to evaluate how the API handles potential rate limiting or overload conditions.

```
#!/bin/bash
API_URL="http://localhost:3000/users"
payload='{
  "username": "rapiduser",
  "email": "rapid@gitforgits.com",
  "password": "RapidPass123",
  "profile": {
    "firstName": "Rapid",
    "lastName": "User",
    "address": {
```

```
            "street": "101 Quick St",
            "city": "Speedville",
            "postalCode": "67890",
            "country": "Testland"
        },
        "contacts": [
            {"type": "mobile", "number": "1112223333"}
        ]
    },
    "settings": {
        "preferences": ["fast", "efficient"],
        "notifications": true
    }
}'
echo "Simulating rapid sequential requests..."
for i in {1..10}; do
  response=$(curl -s -w "\n%{http_code}" -X POST "$API_URL" -H
"Content-Type: application/json" -d "$payload")
  http_code=$(echo "$response" | tail -n1)
  echo "Request $i response code: $http_code"
done
```

This script loops 10 times, sending registration requests in quick succession. Monitoring the responses can help identify if the API imposes rate limits or experiences degradation under a burst of traffic.

All these simulations helped us confirm that the API works well in a lot of different situations and gives clear, actionable error responses when problems arise. These tests make sure that our API does what it's supposed to and stays stable, even when faced with unexpected or difficult situations.

Test Results and Error Debugging

Our testing process might or certainly will reveal some unexpected behavior in our Lumina API that needed practical resolution. So here, we will look into a hands-on debugging where we address two specific issues: an unexpected 200 status code for user registration and a failure in validating the date of birth. We will work through the practical steps to diagnose and fix these problems, making sure the API behaves as intended.

Issue 1: Registration Endpoint Returning 200 Instead 201

During our user registration tests, we noticed that sometimes a POST request would return a 200 status code rather than the expected 201. A quick check of the logs revealed that the endpoint was executing, but the final response wasn't indicating a new resource creation.

So now, to begin its debugging, we first run the registration test with a valid payload and capture the full response:

```
 curl -s -w "\n%{http_code}" -X POST
http://localhost:3000/users \
  -H "Content-Type: application/json" -d '{
    "username": "debuguser",
    "email": "debug@gitforgits.com",
    "password": "DebugPass123",
    "profile": {
      "firstName": "Debug",
      "lastName": "User",
      "address": {
        "street": "100 Debug Ave",
        "city": "Bugsville",
        "postalCode": "11111",
        "country": "Testland"
      },
      "contacts": [
        {"type": "mobile", "number": "1112223333"}
      ]
    },
    "settings": {
```

```
        "preferences": ["alerts"],
        "notifications": true
      }
    }'
```

Notice if the response code is 200 and inspect the body.

Next, we review the inline business logic in the registration endpoint. We need to look for the section where the response is generated. It might resemble:

```
logic: {
  // ... validation and processing steps
  let newUser = db.insert("users", request.body);
  return response(200, {
    id: newUser.id,
    username: newUser.username,
    // other fields...
    createdAt: newUser.createdAt
  });
}
```

The key here is that the function **`response()`** is called with 200 instead of 201.

So now, to resolve the issue, we update the response status code from 200 to 201. The corrected code should be:

```
logic: {
  // ... previous processing steps
  let newUser = db.insert("users", request.body);
  return response(201, {
    id: newUser.id,
    username: newUser.username,
    email: newUser.email,
    profile: newUser.profile,
```

```
    settings: newUser.settings,
    createdAt: newUser.createdAt
  });
}
```

After making this change, we re-run the test to ensure the registration now returns a 201 status code, confirming that the resource creation is correctly communicated.

Issue 2: Date of Birth Validation Failure

Let us consider another test, when a user supplied a date of birth (dob) in an incorrect format, our API failed to handle the error gracefully. Instead of returning a clear 400 error with a descriptive message, it sometimes processed the invalid input, leading to unexpected behavior in downstream operations.

So again, to begin the debugging, we first send a registration request with an incorrectly formatted date of birth:

```
 curl -s -w "\n%{http_code}" -X POST
http://localhost:3000/users \
  -H "Content-Type: application/json" -d '{
    "username": "doberroruser",
    "email": "doberror@gitforgits.com",
    "password": "DobPass123",
    "dob": "31-12-1990",  // Incorrect format; expected YYYY-
MM-DD
    "profile": {
      "firstName": "DOB",
      "lastName": "Error",
      "address": {
        "street": "200 Faulty Rd",
        "city": "Errorville",
        "postalCode": "22222",
        "country": "Testland"
      },
```

```
        "contacts": [
            {"type": "mobile", "number": "2223334444"}
        ]
    },
    "settings": {
        "preferences": ["info"],
        "notifications": false
    }
}'
```

Observe the response—if the API processes the request without flagging the error, our validation logic is insufficient.

Next, look into the section of the endpoint that processes the **dob** field. It might look like this:

```
logic: {
  if (request.body.dob) {
    let parsedDob = datetime.parse(request.body.dob);
    request.body.dob = parsedDob;
  }
  // Continue with user creation...
}
```

Try to figure out that there's no explicit check to see if **parsedDob** is valid.

Now to resolve such issue, you need to enhance the logic to check whether the **dob** is valid after parsing. We update the code to return an error if the parsing fails:

```
logic: {
  if (request.body.dob) {
    let parsedDob = datetime.parse(request.body.dob);
    if (!parsedDob) {
      return error(400, {
        error: "InvalidDateFormat",
```

```
        message: "The date of birth is not in a valid format.
Please use YYYY-MM-DD."
      });
    }
    request.body.dob = parsedDob;
  }
  // Continue with password hashing and further processing...
  request.body.password =
security.hash(request.body.password);
  request.body.createdAt = datetime.now();
  let newUser = db.insert("users", request.body);
  return response(201, {
    id: newUser.id,
    username: newUser.username,
    email: newUser.email,
    profile: newUser.profile,
    settings: newUser.settings,
    createdAt: newUser.createdAt
  });
}
```

By adding this check, any invalid date format will trigger an immediate 400 error with a clear message, preventing further processing of bad data.

After updating the code for both issues:

- Run the registration test again with a correct payload to ensure you receive a 201 status code.
- Re-run the malformed date test to confirm that a 400 error is now returned with the expected error message.

Documenting Debugging Process

Once these errors are fixed, it is beneficial to document the resolutions:

- Note that a 200 response on registration and improper date handling were identified.

- Explain that the status code was updated to 201, and an explicit check for date parsing was added.
- Include these changes in your API documentation and version control commit messages, so future developers understand the rationale behind the fixes.

By engaging with the API in real time and iteratively testing and refining our code, we transformed unexpected behaviors into opportunities for improvement. The process of reproducing errors, reviewing logs and code, isolating faulty components, and applying targeted fixes allowed us to incrementally enhance the reliability of our Lumina API.

Summary

So, here's the gist of what we've learned. We figured out how to thoroughly test our Lumina API using a bunch of automated tests and simulations. We put together these test suites using only the tools we had on hand, which let us simulate stuff like registration, retrieval, updates, and deletions. We made sure each endpoint was responding with the right HTTP status codes and following the set response rules. We sent malformed requests and simulated scenarios like high concurrency, network delays, and unauthorized access to confirm that our error handling was both robust and informative.

We saw discrepancies between the expected and actual outcomes, like the registration endpoint returning an incorrect status code, and identified failures in input validation, like improper handling of date formats. Through iterative testing, we reproduced these errors, examined system logs, and isolated the problematic components within our business logic. Then, we applied fixes like adjusting the response codes and enhancing validation checks to make sure the API responded correctly no matter what. This process showed us how important it is to test and debug continuously when developing APIs.

CHAPTER 6: IMPLEMENTING SECURITY

Overview

This chapter is going to dive into how to implement solid security measures for our Lumina API. First, we'll learn about the different authentication methods Bruno supports and set up JWT authentication to secure user access. Then, we'll take a look at OAuth 2.0, where we'll define detailed authorization rules through scopes and integrate these protocols to control access to sensitive endpoints.

You'll also learn how to manage secrets effectively by storing critical credentials and API keys outside of your system, making sure that sensitive data stays secure throughout the development process. And we'll integrate security testing into our workflow, where you'll simulate common attack scenarios and make sure our API can handle vulnerabilities like SQL injection and unauthorized access. By the time you're done with this chapter, you'll have a solid understanding of how to set up and enforce strong authentication, authorization, and secrets management protocols. You'll also know how to keep an eye on and test your API's security on the regular.

Configuring Authentication Mechanisms

Authentication Methods Overview

Basic Authentication

Basic Authentication is a simple method where the client sends a username and password with every request. These credentials are typically encoded in Base64. Although easy to implement, this method is less secure if not used with HTTPS and is less flexible compared to token-based systems.

API Key Authentication

API Key authentication involves assigning a unique key to each user or application. The key is then passed in the request header or as a query parameter. This method is straightforward but may require additional measures to handle key rotation and storage securely.

JSON Web Token (JWT) Authentication

JWT authentication is a modern, token-based approach where a token is issued after successful login and then sent with subsequent requests. The token contains encoded data, including user identity and permissions, and is digitally signed to prevent tampering. JWT is stateless, scalable, and works well in distributed systems. It offers a balance between security and performance, making it a popular choice for many APIs.

OAuth 2.0

OAuth 2.0 is a robust authorization framework that allows third-party applications to access an API on behalf of a user without exposing user credentials. It is ideal for complex systems and scenarios where multiple permissions and scopes are needed. OAuth 2.0 typically involves multiple flows and requires a dedicated authorization server.

Setting up JWT Authentication

For the Lumina API, we will implement JWT authentication because it offers a secure, stateless mechanism to handle user sessions. JWTs are compact, can be transmitted via URLs or HTTP headers, and allow for decentralized verification. Once a client successfully authenticates, the server issues a JWT that the client uses for subsequent requests. The server verifies the token without having to maintain session state, which simplifies scaling and reduces memory overhead.

Let us now practically learn the process of setting up JWT authentication for our Lumina API.

Define JWT Configuration

Before embedding JWT authentication into our endpoints, we need to set up the configuration. This includes specifying a secret key used for signing tokens, the token expiration time, and any additional options like the algorithm to be used. Typically, these settings are stored in a configuration file that Bruno reads during runtime.

For example, we can create a configuration snippet in our Bruno configuration file, stored at **`~/.bruno/config.json`**:

```
{
  "jwt": {
    "secret": "YourSecureSecretKey",
    "expiresIn": "3600",    // Token valid for 1 hour
    "algorithm": "HS256"
  }
}
```

This configuration tells Bruno to use the HS256 algorithm for signing tokens, with a secret key that should be kept secure, and sets the token expiration to one hour.

Implementing Authentication Endpoint

The next step is to create an authentication endpoint that issues JWTs upon successful login. This endpoint will accept user credentials, validate them, and then generate a JWT if the credentials are correct.

Below is an example of how you might implement this endpoint:

```
// Authentication Endpoint: Login
endpoint /login {
  method: POST;
  request: {
    body: {
      email: string,
      password: string
    }
  };
  logic: {
    // Validate user credentials by checking the database
    let user = db.find("users", { email: request.body.email
});
    if (!user) {
      return error(401, {
        error: "Unauthorized",
        message: "User not found."
      });
    }
    // Verify password (assuming a security.compare function
exists)
    if (!security.compare(request.body.password,
user.password)) {
      return error(401, {
        error: "Unauthorized",
        message: "Invalid credentials."
      });
    }

    // Create the JWT payload with user information
```

```
    let payload = {
      id: user.id,
      email: user.email,
      username: user.username
    };

    // Generate JWT using the secret, expiration, and
algorithm from configuration
    let token = jwt.sign(payload, config.jwt.secret, {
      expiresIn: config.jwt.expiresIn,
      algorithm: config.jwt.algorithm
    });

    // Return the generated token to the client
    return response(200, {
      token: token,
      message: "Authentication successful."
    });
  };
  error: {
    400: {
      error: "InvalidInput",
      message: "Required fields are missing or invalid."
    }
  }
}
```

In this implementation:

- The endpoint accepts a POST request with **`email`** and **`password`** fields.
- The business logic checks whether the user exists and verifies the password using a

hypothetical **security.compare** function.

- Upon successful validation, it builds a payload with essential user information.
- The **jwt.sign** function is used to generate a token using the secret and options defined in our configuration.
- A 200 response is returned along with the JWT, which the client will use for authenticated requests.

Protecting Endpoints with JWT

Once the token issuance is set up, we need to protect other endpoints by verifying the JWT on incoming requests. Typically, this is done via middleware or within the logic of each protected endpoint.

Given below is a quick example of how to integrate token verification in a protected endpoint:

```
// Protected Endpoint: Retrieve User Details
endpoint /users/{id} {
  method: GET;
  request: {
    headers: {
      Authorization: string  // The JWT token should be sent
in the Authorization header
    },
    params: {
      id: number
    }
  };
  logic: {
    // Extract token from the Authorization header
    let authHeader = request.headers.Authorization;
    if (!authHeader || !authHeader.startsWith("Bearer ")) {
      return error(401, {
        error: "Unauthorized",
        message: "Authorization token is missing or invalid."
```

```
    });
  }
  let token = authHeader.split(" ")[1];

  // Verify the token
  let decoded = jwt.verify(token, config.jwt.secret, {
    algorithms: [config.jwt.algorithm]
  });
  if (!decoded) {
    return error(401, {
      error: "Unauthorized",
      message: "Token verification failed."
    });
  }

  // Proceed to fetch user details if token is valid
  let user = db.find("users", { id: request.params.id });
  if (!user) {
    return error(404, {
      error: "NotFound",
      message: "User not found."
    });
  }

  return response(200, {
    id: user.id,
    username: user.username,
    email: user.email,
    profile: user.profile,
```

```
      settings: user.settings,
      createdAt: user.createdAt
    });
  };
  error: {
    400: {
      error: "InvalidInput",
      message: "Missing or invalid parameters."
    }
  }
}
```

In this protected endpoint:

- The API expects a JWT token in the **`Authorization`** header, prefixed with "Bearer ".
- The token is extracted and verified using the **`jwt.verify`** function with the same secret and algorithm.
- If the token is valid, the endpoint proceeds to fetch and return the user details; otherwise, it returns a 401 Unauthorized error.

Testing Authentication Flow

After setting up the authentication and protected endpoints, it is important to test the entire flow:

1. Send a valid login request to **`/login`** and verify that a token is returned. Inspect the token payload (decode it using an online JWT decoder if necessary) to ensure it contains the correct user information.
2. Use the obtained token to access a protected endpoint like **`/users/{id}`**. Confirm that the endpoint returns the correct user data when a valid token is provided and appropriately rejects requests with missing or invalid tokens.
3. Test error cases such as sending an expired token (by manually altering the token's expiration in your test environment) or a token with a wrong signature. Ensure that the API responds with clear and informative error messages.

Testing this flow successfully as taught above, will surely confirm that the API is able to handle both successful and failed authentication scenarios correctly.

Authorization Protocols for API Endpoints

Now that we've got JWT authentication set up, we're expanding our security model by adding OAuth 2.0 to manage authorization for our Lumina API. We know that OAuth 2.0 gives us a solid framework for setting access levels and controlling permissions, making sure that only users or apps with the right permissions can access specific endpoints. So now, we will dive into the OAuth 2.0 concepts, wherein we lay out clear authorization rules using scopes, and show you how to integrate these protocols within our API.

Defining Authorization Scopes

Now before we integrate OAuth 2.0, we need to define the scopes that dictate what parts of the API a client can access. In our Lumina API, we might have scopes such as:

- **read:user:** Allows fetching user data.
- **write:user:** Permits creating, updating, or deleting user data.
- **manage:session:** Grants rights to manage user sessions.

These scopes allow us to establish clear boundaries. For example, a client with only the **`read:user`** scope should not be able to update or delete a user. Clearly defining these rules ensures that access is granular and controlled.

While OAuth 2.0 typically involves a dedicated authorization server, we can simulate the OAuth flow within Bruno for our Lumina API. This simulation will include an endpoint for token issuance and middleware for enforcing scopes on protected endpoints.

Setting up OAuth Configuration

First, add an OAuth configuration to our Bruno settings. This configuration includes parameters such as the client ID, client secret, and defined scopes. In our configuration file, include an OAuth section:

```
{
  "oauth": {
    "clientId": "LuminaClientId",
    "clientSecret": "LuminaSecretKey",
    "scopes": {
      "read:user": "Access to read user data",
      "write:user": "Access to modify user data",
      "manage:session": "Access to manage user sessions"
```

```
    },
    "tokenExpiresIn": "3600"  // 1 hour expiration
  }
}
```

This configuration outlines the parameters our API will use when issuing and validating access tokens.

Creating Token Issuance Endpoint

Next, create an endpoint that simulates the OAuth 2.0 token issuance process. This endpoint, typically **/oauth/token**, will accept client credentials and user login data, then issue an access token with the appropriate scopes as shown below:

```
// OAuth 2.0 Token Issuance Endpoint
endpoint /oauth/token {
  method: POST;
  request: {
    body: {
      clientId: string,
      clientSecret: string,
      email: string,
      password: string,
      scope: string  // Requested scope, e.g., "read:user
write:user"
    }
  };
  logic: {
    // Verify client credentials against configuration
    if (request.body.clientId != config.oauth.clientId ||
request.body.clientSecret != config.oauth.clientSecret) {
      return error(401, {
        error: "Unauthorized",
```

```
        message: "Invalid client credentials."
      });
    }
    // Authenticate user using existing logic
    let user = db.find("users", { email: request.body.email
});
    if (!user || !security.compare(request.body.password,
user.password)) {
      return error(401, {
        error: "Unauthorized",
        message: "Invalid user credentials."
      });
    }
    // Validate requested scope: ensure it is a subset of
allowed scopes
    let requestedScopes = request.body.scope.split(" ");
    for (let i = 0; i < requestedScopes.length; i++) {
      if
(!config.oauth.scopes.hasOwnProperty(requestedScopes[i])) {
        return error(400, {
          error: "InvalidScope",
          message: "The requested scope " + requestedScopes[i]
+ " is not permitted."
        });
      }
    }
    // Create JWT payload for OAuth token including scope and
user details
    let payload = {
      id: user.id,
      email: user.email,
```

```
      username: user.username,
      scope: requestedScopes.join(" ")
    };
    // Generate OAuth token with JWT signing using OAuth
configuration
    let token = jwt.sign(payload, config.oauth.clientSecret, {
      expiresIn: config.oauth.tokenExpiresIn,
      algorithm: config.jwt.algorithm  // Reuse JWT algorithm
setting
    });
    return response(200, {
      access_token: token,
      token_type: "Bearer",
      expires_in: config.oauth.tokenExpiresIn,
      scope: requestedScopes.join(" ")
    });
  };
  error: {
    400: {
      error: "InvalidInput",
      message: "Missing or invalid request parameters."
    }
  }
}
```

In this endpoint:

- The client provides their **clientId**, **clientSecret**, along with the user's **email** and **password**, and the desired scope.
- We first verify the client credentials against our configuration.
- Next, we authenticate the user using our existing logic.
- We then validate that the requested scope is allowed.

- If everything checks out, we create a JWT that includes the user's identity and the approved scope.
- Finally, the token is returned with a response containing token details.

Enforcing Authorization in Protected Endpoints

Once an access token is issued, it must be validated on protected endpoints. The access token should contain the scope information, and each endpoint should enforce that only clients with the appropriate scope can access it.

Let us consider a protected endpoint that requires the **`write:user`** scope:

```
// Protected Endpoint: Updating User Details with Scope Check
endpoint /users/{id} {
  method: PUT;
  request: {
    headers: {
      Authorization: string  // Bearer token
    },
    params: {
      id: number
    },
    body: {
      // Fields to update
      username: string?,
      email: string?,
      profile: {  // Optional profile updates
        firstName: string?,
        lastName: string?,
        address: {
          street: string?,
          city: string?,
          postalCode: string?,
```

```
        country: string?
      }?
    }?
  }
};
logic: {
  // Extract and verify the access token from the
Authorization header
  let authHeader = request.headers.Authorization;
  if (!authHeader || !authHeader.startsWith("Bearer ")) {
    return error(401, {
      error: "Unauthorized",
      message: "Authorization token is missing or invalid."
    });
  }
  let token = authHeader.split(" ")[1];
  let decoded = jwt.verify(token, config.oauth.clientSecret,
{
    algorithms: [config.jwt.algorithm]
  });
  if (!decoded) {
    return error(401, {
      error: "Unauthorized",
      message: "Token verification failed."
    });
  }
  // Check if the token contains the required scope for
updating user details
  let tokenScopes = decoded.scope.split(" ");
  if (!tokenScopes.includes("write:user")) {
```

```
      return error(403, {
        error: "Forbidden",
        message: "Insufficient scope to update user details."
      });
    }
    // Proceed with updating the user information
    let user = db.find("users", { id: request.params.id });
    if (!user) {
      return error(404, {
        error: "NotFound",
        message: "User not found."
      });
    }

    // Update user data (simplified for demonstration)
    let updatedUser = db.update("users", { id: user.id },
request.body);

    return response(200, {
      id: updatedUser.id,
      username: updatedUser.username,
      email: updatedUser.email,
      profile: updatedUser.profile,
      updatedAt: updatedUser.updatedAt
    });
  };
  error: {
    400: {
      error: "InvalidInput",
```

```
      message: "Missing or invalid parameters."
    }
  }
}
```

This endpoint illustrates how to enforce authorization rules:

- It extracts the access token from the **Authorization** header.
- The token is verified using the client secret and the appropriate algorithm.
- The endpoint checks whether the token's scope includes **write:user**.
- If the scope is insufficient, it returns a 403 Forbidden error.
- Otherwise, it processes the update request and returns the updated user information.

With this, we successfully defined clear authorization rules through scopes and demonstrated a practical implementation wherein we set up an endpoint to issue access tokens and protected other endpoints by enforcing scope checks.

Secrets Management

Our application's security depends on keeping sensitive data like database passwords, client secrets, and encryption keys under lock and key. If these credentials are exposed, an attacker could gain unauthorized access to the system, compromising data integrity and user privacy. So, proper secrets management involves more than just storing these credentials securely. It also involves controlling access to them and rotating them regularly.

Secure Storage Techniques

Environment Variables

A common strategy for managing secrets is to store them in environment variables rather than hardcoding them into the source code. Environment variables keep sensitive data outside of the codebase and allow for different values in development, testing, and production environments. In our Lumina API project, we use environment variables to store secrets such as the JWT secret, OAuth client secrets, and database connection strings.

For example, you might add the following lines to your shell configuration file:

```
export LUMINA_JWT_SECRET="YourSuperSecretJWTKey"
export LUMINA_OAUTH_CLIENT_SECRET="YourOAuthSecretKey"
```

```
export LUMINA_DB_PASSWORD="YourDatabasePassword"
```

By doing this, our application can retrieve these secrets at runtime without the risk of accidentally committing them to version control.

Secrets Files and Vaults

For enhanced security, especially in production environments, using a dedicated secrets management tool or vault is advisable. There are tools like HashiCorp Vault, AWS Secrets Manager, or Azure Key Vault that can provide secure storage, access controls, and auditing capabilities. While our live learning environment may not include these external tools, it is important to understand that they allow dynamic retrieval of secrets through secure APIs.

A common approach is to have a local secrets file (e.g., **`secrets.json`**) that is kept outside the version control system. This file can be structured as follows:

```
{
  "jwtSecret": "YourSuperSecretJWTKey",
  "oauthClientSecret": "YourOAuthSecretKey",
  "dbPassword": "YourDatabasePassword"
}
```

Now here, we have to make sure to include this file in your **`.gitignore`** to prevent it from being committed to your repository.

Integrating Secrets

Loading Environment Variables

In our API configuration files, we can reference these variables directly. For example, in our **`config.json`**, instead of hardcoding the secret key, we might include a reference like this:

```
{
  "jwt": {
    "secret": "$LUMINA_JWT_SECRET",
    "expiresIn": "3600",
    "algorithm": "HS256"
  },
  "oauth": {
```

```
        "clientId": "LuminaClientId",
        "clientSecret": "$LUMINA_OAUTH_CLIENT_SECRET",
        "scopes": {
          "read:user": "Access to read user data",
          "write:user": "Access to modify user data",
          "manage:session": "Access to manage user sessions"
        },
        "tokenExpiresIn": "3600"
      },
      "database": {
        "password": "$LUMINA_DB_PASSWORD"
      }
    }
```

When Bruno starts, it will substitute the environment variable values accordingly, ensuring that secrets remain external to the codebase.

Securing API Keys and Credentials

Only trusted components of the application should have permission to access these secrets. In our Lumina API, this means ensuring that endpoints that require authentication or access to sensitive data are properly secured and that secret values are not exposed in logs or error messages. So for example, when a login endpoint generates a JWT, the secret used for signing should never be included in the output or logs. Similarly, when connecting to a database, error messages should be sanitized to avoid revealing connection details.

Sample Program: Secrets Management in Practice

We will walk through a practical example of implementing secrets management in our Lumina API project. Suppose we have an endpoint that requires database access. Instead of hardcoding the database password in our code, we use an environment variable.

So here, first ensure that the following variables are set in your shell:

```
export LUMINA_DB_PASSWORD="YourDatabasePassword"
```

Next, in your Bruno configuration file (**`config.json`**), we will reference the variable:

```
{
```

```
  "database": {
    "password": "$LUMINA_DB_PASSWORD"
  }
}
```

Next, in the business logic where you need to connect to the database, we will retrieve the password from the configuration:

```
logic: {
  let dbPassword = config.database.password;
  // Use dbPassword to connect securely to the database
  let connection = db.connect({
    host: "db.gitforgits.com",
    user: "dbuser",
    password: dbPassword,
    database: "lumina"
  });
  // Continue with API operations...
}
```

If you follow these steps, the secret stays out of sight and is only accessed when needed, reducing the risk of exposure.

Integrating Security Testing

Opportunities of Vulnerabilities

Throughout the API lifecycle, vulnerabilities can be introduced or discovered during different phases. Given below are some key phases:

- Design and Architecture

At the outset, the API design itself may have flaws. This can include overly permissive endpoint structures, lack of proper authentication and authorization, or poorly defined data schemas that can be exploited. Vulnerabilities here may lead to issues such as insecure data exposure or injection attacks.

- Development and Coding

During development, bugs and misconfigurations in business logic, error handling, and data validation can create security weaknesses. Inadequate input sanitization or incorrect use of cryptographic functions are common pitfalls. It is in this phase that most coding errors occur, which could potentially be exploited by attackers.

- Testing and Quality Assurance

Automated testing often focuses on functionality, but integrating security tests during this phase can uncover issues like incorrect permission settings, inadequate error responses, or insufficient logging. Security testing tools and scripts help simulate attacks and measure the API's resilience.

- Deployment and Configuration

Once the API is deployed, misconfigured environments, such as improperly set environment variables or unsecured endpoints, may introduce vulnerabilities. Security testing in this phase ensures that the deployment environment adheres to best practices, such as secure communication protocols and strict access controls.

- Maintenance and Monitoring

Even after deployment, continuous monitoring is essential. Vulnerabilities may be discovered over time due to evolving threat landscapes, changes in dependencies, or new integration points. Ongoing security tests and audits help maintain a robust defense posture.

Incorporating Simple Security Tests

Now to integrate security testing into our Lumina API, we can use our pre-installed command-line tools to simulate common attack scenarios. In the below, we will have a simple security test that checks for potential vulnerabilities in endpoint authorization and data validation.

Test 1: SQL Injection Simulation

A common vulnerability in APIs is SQL injection. Although our API uses secure data handling practices, it is essential to test if it properly sanitizes inputs. We can simulate an SQL injection attempt by sending a malicious payload to an endpoint and verifying that it does not compromise our data integrity.

Below is a sample shell script that simulates an SQL injection attempt on a hypothetical search endpoint (e.g., **/users/search**):

```
#!/bin/bash
API_URL="http://localhost:3000/users/search"
MALICIOUS_PAYLOAD='{"query": "testuser\' OR \'1\'=\'1"}'
```

```
response=$(curl -s -w "\n%{http_code}" -X POST "$API_URL" -H
"Content-Type: application/json" -d "$MALICIOUS_PAYLOAD")
http_body=$(echo "$response" | sed '$d')
http_code=$(echo "$response" | tail -n1)
if [ "$http_code" -eq 400 ] || [ "$http_code" -eq 404 ]; then
  echo "SQL Injection test passed. Status code: $http_code"
else
  echo "SQL Injection test failed. Status code: $http_code"
  echo "Response: $http_body"
fi
```

In this script, we send a POST request with a payload designed to manipulate a potential SQL query. A robust API should sanitize this input, resulting in either a 400 or 404 error, indicating that the malicious input was not processed. If the API returns a 200 status or unexpected data, that indicates a vulnerability that must be addressed.

Test 2: Unauthorized Access Check

Another critical security test is to ensure that endpoints requiring authentication are protected against unauthorized access. Here, we simulate this by making a request to a protected endpoint without proper authorization headers and verifying that the API returns a 401 Unauthorized response.

```
#!/bin/bash
# Define the protected endpoint, e.g., updating user details
API_URL="http://localhost:3000/users/1"
PAYLOAD='{"username": "unauthorizedUpdate"}'
response=$(curl -s -w "\n%{http_code}" -X PUT "$API_URL" -H
"Content-Type: application/json" -d "$PAYLOAD")
http_code=$(echo "$response" | tail -n1)
if [ "$http_code" -eq 401 ]; then
  echo "Unauthorized access test passed. Status code:
$http_code"
else
```

```
  echo "Unauthorized access test failed. Status code:
$http_code"
fi
```

This script sends a PUT request without the necessary authorization token. A proper security implementation should reject this request with a 401 status code, confirming that the endpoint is protected.

Test 3: Input Validation Robustness

We also need to ensure that our API correctly handles unexpected or malformed input. For instance, if an endpoint expects a numerical value but receives a string, the API should return a 400 error.

Following is a script that tests input validation:

```
#!/bin/bash
# Define the endpoint for updating a user
API_URL="http://localhost:3000/users/1"
INVALID_PAYLOAD='{"username": "testuser", "email": "not-an-
email"}'
response=$(curl -s -w "\n%{http_code}" -X PUT "$API_URL" -H
"Content-Type: application/json" -d "$INVALID_PAYLOAD")
http_body=$(echo "$response" | sed '$d')
http_code=$(echo "$response" | tail -n1)
if [ "$http_code" -eq 400 ]; then
  echo "Input validation test passed. Status code: $http_code"
  echo "Error details: $(echo "$http_body" | grep -o
'"message":"[^"]*' | awk -F: '{print $2}' | tr -d '"')"
else
  echo "Input validation test failed. Status code: $http_code"
  echo "Response: $http_body"
fi
```

This test submits an invalid email format in a user update request. The expected response is a 400 error with a descriptive message, confirming that the API properly validates inputs.

Integrating Security Tests into the Workflow

Now, once individual security tests are defined, try to integrate them into your overall testing workflow. This can be simply done by creating a master security test script that sequentially runs each test case and summarizes the results.

See the following sample master security test script:

```
#!/bin/bash
echo "Starting security tests for Lumina API..."
# Run SQL Injection simulation
echo "Running SQL Injection Test..."
./test_sql_injection.sh
# Run Unauthorized Access check
echo "Running Unauthorized Access Test..."
./test_unauthorized_access.sh
# Run Input Validation Test
echo "Running Input Validation Test..."
./test_input_validation.sh
echo "Security tests completed."
```

If you automate these tests and add them to your CI/CD pipeline, you can be sure that every change to your API is checked right away for any potential security problems. This is a good way to make sure your API is always secure, and it also helps everyone to keep improving their security practices.

Summary

With all that in mind, we made some changes to the security framework of our Lumina API. We explored different authentication methods in Bruno and chose JWT because it offered a good balance of security and scalability. We set up an authentication endpoint that issues secure tokens upon successful login.

Then, we added OAuth 2.0 to our security model, defining specific authorization scopes like read, write, and session management. At the same time, we dealt with the handling of sensitive information through proper secrets management techniques. We moved some of our data, like client secrets and database credentials, to environment variables, so they weren't hardcoded in our source code and there was less risk of exposure. We also integrated security testing into our development workflow by simulating common attack scenarios, like SQL injection attempts and unauthorized access. Overall, the chapter really reinforced our understanding of security best practices and showed us a proactive, layered approach to protecting our API from potential threats.

CHAPTER 7: DEBUGGING AND OPTIMIZING APIs

Overview

In this chapter, we will delve into the world of debugging and optimizing our Lumina API using Bruno's powerful tools. You will learn to analyze API interactions live, tracing the complete flow of requests and responses to understand how data moves through each endpoint. We will explore the use of real-time breakpoints, variable inspections, and detailed logging to uncover bottlenecks and identify errors.

Throughout this chapter, you will see practical examples of how to set up and use these debugging features to monitor performance, diagnose issues, and fine-tune your API. We will also cover techniques for capturing critical performance metrics, ensuring that each operation from data normalization to database insertion is logged and tracked efficiently.

Live Analysis of API Interactions

In this topic, we will explore the Bruno's debugging features wherein we will learn to perform live analysis of API interactions within our Lumina API. We will cover three scenarios: user registration, user retrieval with token verification, and high concurrency performance testing, all while actively using Bruno's live debugging capabilities.

Now here, before we jump into the scenarios, we need to check that our Bruno environment is running in debug mode. To do like this, you can start Bruno with a debug flag, like so:

```
bruno start --debug
```

This command enables live logging, breakpoints, and real-time variable inspection. As you run your API interactions, Bruno will output detailed logs directly in your terminal.

Scenario 1: Live Debugging User Registration

We will begin with the user registration endpoint. We want to see the entire flow—from receiving the request to processing business logic and generating a response.

Run Registration Test with Debugging Enabled

Create a shell script named **debug_registration.sh**:

```
#!/bin/bash
API_URL="http://localhost:3000/users"
PAYLOAD='{
  "username": "debuguser",
  "email": "debug@gitforgits.com",
```

```
  "password": "DebugPass123",
  "profile": {
    "firstName": "Debug",
    "lastName": "User",
    "address": {
      "street": "100 Debug Ave",
      "city": "Bugsville",
      "postalCode": "11111",
      "country": "Testland"
    },
    "contacts": [
      {"type": "mobile", "number": "1112223333"}
    ]
  },
  "settings": {
    "preferences": ["alerts"],
    "notifications": true
  }
}'
echo "Sending user registration request..."
response=$(curl -s -w "\n%{http_code}" -X POST "$API_URL" -H
"Content-Type: application/json" -d "$PAYLOAD")
http_body=$(echo "$response" | sed '$d')
http_code=$(echo "$response" | tail -n1)
echo "Response code: $http_code"
echo "Response body: $http_body"
```

You need to make the script executable:

```
chmod +x debug_registration.sh
```

Set Breakpoint for Registration Logic

Within your Bru Lang file defining the **/users** endpoint, add a breakpoint at the point where critical business logic occurs as below:

```
endpoint /users {
  method: POST;
  request: { ... },
  logic: {
    // Set a breakpoint before processing the registration
    bruno.debug.setBreakpoint("user_registration_start");
    // Normalize email and hash password
    request.body.email = request.body.email.toLowerCase();
    request.body.password =
security.hash(request.body.password);
    // Set creation timestamp
    request.body.createdAt = datetime.now();
    // Insert new user record into the database
    let newUser = db.insert("users", request.body);
    // Return response with 201 status
    return response(201, {
      id: newUser.id,
      username: newUser.username,
      email: newUser.email,
      profile: newUser.profile,
      settings: newUser.settings,
      createdAt: newUser.createdAt
    });
  };
  error: { ... }
}
```

When you run **./debug_registration.sh**, Bruno will pause execution at the breakpoint **user_registration_start**. In your terminal, use Bruno's interactive console to inspect variables:

```
bruno.debug.inspect request.body
```

This command displays the contents of **request.body** in real time, so you can verify that the email is normalized and the password is hashed correctly.

Scenario 2: Debugging User Retrieval and Token Verification

Next, we want to debug the user retrieval endpoint, which requires token verification. This scenario allows you to see how Bruno logs the extraction and verification of JWT tokens.

Create Retrieval Test Script

Create a file named **debug_retrieval.sh**:

```
#!/bin/bash
# Assuming you have a valid token from the login process
TOKEN="your_valid_jwt_token_here"
USER_ID=1
API_URL="http://localhost:3000/users/$USER_ID"
echo "Sending user retrieval request..."
response=$(curl -s -w "\n%{http_code}" -X GET "$API_URL" -H
"Content-Type: application/json" -H "Authorization: Bearer
$TOKEN")
http_body=$(echo "$response" | sed '$d')
http_code=$(echo "$response" | tail -n1)
echo "Response code: $http_code"
echo "Response body: $http_body"
```

Now, as usual, make the script executable:

```
chmod +x debug_retrieval.sh
```

Insert Debugging Commands

In your Bru Lang file for **/users/{id}**, add debugging commands to inspect the token verification process:

```
endpoint /users/{id} {
  method: GET;
  request: {
    headers: { Authorization: string },
    params: { id: number }
  };
  logic: {
    bruno.debug.setBreakpoint("token_verification_start");
    // Extract token from Authorization header
    let authHeader = request.headers.Authorization;
    if (!authHeader || !authHeader.startsWith("Bearer ")) {
      return error(401, {
        error: "Unauthorized",
        message: "Missing or invalid token."
      });
    }
    let token = authHeader.split(" ")[1];
    // Verify the token
    let decoded = jwt.verify(token, config.oauth.clientSecret,
{
      algorithms: [config.jwt.algorithm]
    });
    if (!decoded) {
      return error(401, {
        error: "Unauthorized",
        message: "Token verification failed."
      });
    }
```

```
    // Log the decoded token for debugging
    bruno.debug.log("Decoded Token: ", decoded);
    // Fetch user details from database
    let user = db.find("users", { id: request.params.id });
    if (!user) {
      return error(404, {
        error: "NotFound",
        message: "User not found."
      });
    }

    return response(200, {
      id: user.id,
      username: user.username,
      email: user.email,
      profile: user.profile,
      settings: user.settings,
      createdAt: user.createdAt
    });
  };
  error: { ... }
}
```

When running **./debug_retrieval.sh**, the execution pauses at **token_verification_start**. After this, make use of the debugging console to inspect **authHeader** and check the log message for "Decoded Token:" to confirm that the JWT is correctly parsed.

Scenario 3: High Concurrency Analysis with Debug Logging

Now the final scenario is to test the performance under high load, for which we will simulate multiple simultaneous registration requests and analyze performance metrics.

Create High Concurrency Test Script

At first, we will create a script named **debug_high_concurrency.sh**:

```
#!/bin/bash
API_URL="http://localhost:3000/users"
PAYLOAD_TEMPLATE='{
  "username": "user%d",
  "email": "user%d@gitforgits.com",
  "password": "ConcurrentPass123",
  "profile": {
    "firstName": "User",
    "lastName": "Concurrent",
    "address": {
      "street": "123 Concurrency Blvd",
      "city": "Loadtown",
      "postalCode": "99999",
      "country": "Testland"
    },
    "contacts": [
      {"type": "mobile", "number": "1234567890"}
    ]
  },
  "settings": {
    "preferences": ["fast", "efficient"],
    "notifications": true
  }
}'
simulate_request() {
  local i=$1
```

```
  local payload=$(printf "$PAYLOAD_TEMPLATE" "$i" "$i")
  local response=$(curl -s -w "\n%{http_code}" -X POST
"$API_URL" -H "Content-Type: application/json" -d "$payload")
  local http_code=$(echo "$response" | tail -n1)
  echo "User $i registration response code: $http_code"
}
echo "Starting high concurrency test..."
for i in {1..50}; do
  simulate_request $i &
done
wait
echo "High concurrency test completed."
```

As usual, we need to make the script executable:

```
chmod +x debug_high_concurrency.sh
```

Analyze Live Logs for Performance Metrics

Now here, the Bruno's live logging will capture:

- The timestamp of each incoming request.
- Execution times for each critical operation (e.g., data validation, database insertion).
- Any errors or delays encountered.

We now need to set a breakpoint in the registration endpoint to capture performance metrics, such as before and after the database insertion:

```
endpoint /users {
  method: POST;
  request: { ... },
  logic: {
    // Log the start time
    let startTime = datetime.now();
    bruno.debug.log("Registration start time: ", startTime);
```

```
    // Process the registration
    request.body.email = request.body.email.toLowerCase();
    request.body.password =
security.hash(request.body.password);
    request.body.createdAt = datetime.now();
    // Set a breakpoint before database insertion for
performance analysis
    bruno.debug.setBreakpoint("db_insertion_start");
    let newUser = db.insert("users", request.body);
    // Log the end time and calculate duration
    let endTime = datetime.now();
    bruno.debug.log("Registration end time: ", endTime);
    let duration = datetime.diff(endTime, startTime);
    bruno.debug.log("Registration processing duration (ms): ",
duration);
    return response(201, {
      id: newUser.id,
      username: newUser.username,
      email: newUser.email,
      profile: newUser.profile,
      settings: newUser.settings,
      createdAt: newUser.createdAt
    });
  };
  error: { ... }
}
```

When running the high concurrency script, use Bruno's debug console to check the logged start times, end times, and calculated durations. This live performance data helps you identify any bottlenecks or spikes in processing times.

With all the above three scenarios, you are actively testing, observing, and refining your API in a live environment. Every scenario provides immediate feedback that you can use to optimize your

API's performance and reliability.

Tracing API Requests and Responses

Tracing allows us to see the complete cycle of a request. It involves capturing:

- **Incoming Request Data:** The exact payload and headers that hit the endpoint.
- **Intermediate Processing:** Key transformations, validations, and business logic steps.
- **Outgoing Response Data:** The final output sent back to the client, including status codes and response bodies.

All these stages verify that the data is correctly processed at every layer.

Implementing Tracing

So, let us begin with the tracing. Here, to integrate tracing into our endpoints, we need to enhance our Bru Lang definitions with logging statements at critical points. We will incorporate tracing into our user registration endpoint as an example.

Below is a sample implementation of the user registration endpoint with detailed trace logs:

```
endpoint /users {
  method: POST;
  request: {
    body: {
      username: string,
      email: string,
      password: string,
      profile: {
        firstName: string,
        lastName: string,
        address: {
          street: string,
          city: string,
          postalCode: string,
          country: string
```

```
      },
      contacts: [
        {
          type: string,
          number: string
        }
      ],
      socialMedia?: {
        twitter: string?,
        facebook: string?,
        instagram: string?
      }
    },
    settings: {
      preferences: [string],
      notifications: boolean
    }
  }
};
logic: {
  // Trace the incoming request body
  bruno.debug.log("Incoming Request:", request.body);

  // Normalize email and log the change
  request.body.email = request.body.email.toLowerCase();
  bruno.debug.log("Normalized Email:", request.body.email);

  // Hash the password and trace the operation (without
revealing the actual password)
```

```
    let originalPassword = request.body.password;
    request.body.password =
security.hash(request.body.password);
    bruno.debug.log("Password hashed. Original:",
originalPassword, "Hashed:", request.body.password);

    // Set creation timestamp and log it
    request.body.createdAt = datetime.now();
    bruno.debug.log("Timestamp set at:",
request.body.createdAt);

    // Set a breakpoint before database insertion to inspect
data
    bruno.debug.setBreakpoint("before_db_insertion");

    // Insert new user record into the database
    let newUser = db.insert("users", request.body);
    bruno.debug.log("User inserted into database:", newUser);

    // Prepare response and log the final output
    let responsePayload = {
      id: newUser.id,
      username: newUser.username,
      email: newUser.email,
      profile: newUser.profile,
      settings: newUser.settings,
      createdAt: newUser.createdAt
    };
    bruno.debug.log("Response Payload:", responsePayload);
```

```
    return response(201, responsePayload);
  };
  error: {
    400: {
      error: "InvalidInput",
      message: "Required fields are missing or contain invalid
data."
    }
  }
}
```

Here,

- We log the full request payload as soon as it arrives.
- Each transformation step is logged so we can see the effect of our processing without exposing sensitive information.
- A breakpoint (**before_db_insertion**) is set right before the database operation. This allows you to pause the execution and inspect all data, ensuring that everything is as expected.
- Before returning the response, the payload is logged, which helps in confirming that the response adheres to our defined schema.

Sample Program: Tracing User Retrieval

We will apply similar tracing to our user retrieval endpoint, which is protected by token verification. Following is how you can implement detailed tracing for that endpoint:

```
endpoint /users/{id} {
  method: GET;
  request: {
    headers: {
      Authorization: string
    },
    params: {
      id: number
```

```
    }
  };
  logic: {
    bruno.debug.log("Incoming Request Headers:",
request.headers);
    bruno.debug.log("Request Params:", request.params);
    // Extract token and log the process
    let authHeader = request.headers.Authorization;
    if (!authHeader || !authHeader.startsWith("Bearer ")) {
      return error(401, {
        error: "Unauthorized",
        message: "Missing or invalid token."
      });
    }
    let token = authHeader.split(" ")[1];
    bruno.debug.log("Extracted Token:", token);
    // Verify token and log the decoded result
    let decoded = jwt.verify(token, config.oauth.clientSecret,
{
      algorithms: [config.jwt.algorithm]
    });
    if (!decoded) {
      return error(401, {
        error: "Unauthorized",
        message: "Token verification failed."
      });
    }
    bruno.debug.log("Decoded Token:", decoded);
    // Fetch user details from the database and log the result
    let user = db.find("users", { id: request.params.id });
```

```
    if (!user) {
      return error(404, {
        error: "NotFound",
        message: "User not found."
      });
    }
    bruno.debug.log("Fetched User Data:", user);
    return response(200, {
      id: user.id,
      username: user.username,
      email: user.email,
      profile: user.profile,
      settings: user.settings,
      createdAt: user.createdAt
    });
  };
  error: {
    400: {
      error: "InvalidInput",
      message: "Missing or invalid parameters."
    }
  }
}
```

In this retrieval endpoint:

- The incoming headers and parameters are logged to verify the data provided by the client.
- Each step in the token extraction and verification process is logged, including the decoded token.
- After fetching the user data, the retrieved information is logged. This gives you a clear trail of how data is fetched and transformed before forming the final response.

Once you run these endpoints, the trace logs will appear in your Bruno debug console. We can verify that the timestamps on your logs match the expected flow. For example, the creation timestamp should be close to the current time when the registration request is made.

We can confirm that the variables like **`request.body.email`** and **`request.body.password`** have been transformed correctly. The hashed password should be different from the original input. Similarly, when execution halts at a breakpoint, inspect the current state of all relevant variables to confirm that the data is correctly structured before performing critical operations such as database insertions.

All this live tracing not only helps in confirming that your data transformations and business logic are functioning correctly but also gives us or builds within us a confidence to spot any unexpected behavior or performance bottlenecks in our API.

Implementing Logging

Logs are a key part of monitoring and debugging our Lumina API. With Bruno's logging features, we can record every important action within our API, track performance, and capture detailed error information. What we're going to do here is show you how to set up logging in our setup and integrate logging commands into our API endpoints. That way, we can make sure that all major operations are documented in real time.

Configuring Logging

Bruno's logging system can be configured through a dedicated section in our configuration file. This configuration sets the log level, specifies output formats, and directs log outputs to appropriate destinations such as the console or log files.

In our Bruno configuration file, we define a logging section:

```
{
  "logging": {
    "level": "debug",          // Levels: debug, info, warn,
error
    "format": "json",          // Format can be json, plain, or
custom
    "output": "console"        // Options: console, file, or
both
  },
  "jwt": {
```

```
    "secret": "$LUMINA_JWT_SECRET",
    "expiresIn": "3600",
    "algorithm": "HS256"
  },
  "oauth": {
    "clientId": "LuminaClientId",
    "clientSecret": "$LUMINA_OAUTH_CLIENT_SECRET",
    "scopes": {
      "read:user": "Access to read user data",
      "write:user": "Access to modify user data",
      "manage:session": "Access to manage user sessions"
    },
    "tokenExpiresIn": "3600"
  },
  "database": {
    "password": "$LUMINA_DB_PASSWORD"
  }
}
```

This configuration instructs Bruno to log messages at the "debug" level, ensuring detailed output. The logs are formatted in JSON for structured analysis and are printed to the console for immediate review.

Integrating Logging in API Endpoints

When we integrate logging within our endpoints, it's key to tracing the flow of data and tracking important events. We can insert logging commands directly into the logic blocks of our Bru Lang files, which lets us capture every step of the process, from input validation to business logic execution and database interactions.

Logging in User Registration

Consider the user registration endpoint where we want to log key actions:

```
endpoint /users {
```

```
method: POST;
request: {
  body: {
    username: string,
    email: string,
    password: string,
    profile: {
      firstName: string,
      lastName: string,
      address: {
        street: string,
        city: string,
        postalCode: string,
        country: string
      },
      contacts: [
        {
          type: string,
          number: string
        }
      ],
      socialMedia?: {
        twitter: string?,
        facebook: string?,
        instagram: string?
      }
    },
    settings: {
      preferences: [string],
```

```
        notifications: boolean
      }
    }
  };
  logic: {
    // Log the incoming request details
    bruno.debug.log("Incoming Request Payload:",
request.body);
    // Normalize email and log the result
    request.body.email = request.body.email.toLowerCase();
    bruno.debug.log("Normalized Email:", request.body.email);
    // Hash the password and log the transformation (without
revealing sensitive details)
    let originalPassword = request.body.password;
    request.body.password =
security.hash(request.body.password);
    bruno.debug.log("Password hashed. Original length:",
originalPassword.length, "Hashed:", request.body.password);
    // Set the creation timestamp and log it
    request.body.createdAt = datetime.now();
    bruno.debug.log("Timestamp Set:", request.body.createdAt);
    // Set a debug checkpoint before inserting into the
database
    bruno.debug.setBreakpoint("before_db_insertion");
    // Insert new user into the database and log the result
    let newUser = db.insert("users", request.body);
    bruno.debug.log("User Inserted:", newUser);
    // Prepare response payload and log it
    let responsePayload = {
      id: newUser.id,
      username: newUser.username,
```

```
      email: newUser.email,
      profile: newUser.profile,
      settings: newUser.settings,
      createdAt: newUser.createdAt
    };
    bruno.debug.log("Response Payload:", responsePayload);
    return response(201, responsePayload);
  };
  error: {
    400: {
      error: "InvalidInput",
      message: "Required fields are missing or contain invalid
data."
    }
  }
}
```

In the above script,

- We log the full payload immediately to confirm what data the endpoint is receiving.
- After normalizing the email and hashing the password, logs capture these transformations without exposing the sensitive raw values.
- The timestamp is recorded to have a reference point for performance tracking.
- A breakpoint is set before database insertion to pause execution for in-depth inspection if needed.
- The final response payload is also logged to verify that the output conforms to our expected structure.

Logging in Protected Endpoints

For endpoints that require token verification, logging becomes essential for security auditing. Let us consider the user retrieval endpoint now where the token is extracted and verified:

```
endpoint /users/{id} {
  method: GET;
```

```
  request: {
    headers: {
      Authorization: string
    },
    params: {
      id: number
    }
  };
  logic: {
    // Log the incoming headers and parameters
    bruno.debug.log("Incoming Headers:", request.headers);
    bruno.debug.log("Request Parameters:", request.params);
    // Extract token and log the extraction process
    let authHeader = request.headers.Authorization;
    if (!authHeader || !authHeader.startsWith("Bearer ")) {
      return error(401, {
        error: "Unauthorized",
        message: "Missing or invalid token."
      });
    }
    let token = authHeader.split(" ")[1];
    bruno.debug.log("Extracted Token:", token);
    // Verify token and log the decoded information
    let decoded = jwt.verify(token, config.oauth.clientSecret,
{
      algorithms: [config.jwt.algorithm]
    });
    if (!decoded) {
      return error(401, {
```

```
        error: "Unauthorized",
        message: "Token verification failed."
      });
    }
    bruno.debug.log("Decoded Token:", decoded);
    // Fetch user details from the database and log the
retrieved data
    let user = db.find("users", { id: request.params.id });
    if (!user) {
      return error(404, {
        error: "NotFound",
        message: "User not found."
      });
    }
    bruno.debug.log("Fetched User Data:", user);
    return response(200, {
      id: user.id,
      username: user.username,
      email: user.email,
      profile: user.profile,
      settings: user.settings,
      createdAt: user.createdAt
    });
  };
  error: {
    400: {
      error: "InvalidInput",
      message: "Missing or invalid parameters."
    }
```

```
  }
}
```

Now here,

- Logs capture the exact headers and parameters received.
- The token is logged at each stage—extraction and after decoding to pinpoint any issues in the authentication process.
- The result of the user lookup is logged that helps to verify the data returned from the database meets expectations.

Performance Tracking via Logs

Robust logging isn't just for error debugging; it also helps track performance. By logging execution times and key variable states, you can analyze which parts of your API may be causing delays. For instance, you can add logs to capture the duration of specific operations:

```
logic: {
  let startTime = datetime.now();
  bruno.debug.log("Start Time:", startTime);
  // Perform a critical operation, such as database insertion
  let newUser = db.insert("users", request.body);
  let endTime = datetime.now();
  bruno.debug.log("End Time:", endTime);
  let duration = datetime.diff(endTime, startTime);
  bruno.debug.log("Operation Duration (ms):", duration);
  // Continue with response construction
  return response(201, {
    id: newUser.id,
    username: newUser.username,
    email: newUser.email,
    profile: newUser.profile,
    settings: newUser.settings,
    createdAt: newUser.createdAt
```

```
  });
}
```

This snippet logs the start and end times of the database insertion process, calculating the duration. Such logs help you identify slow operations and optimize them accordingly.

Customizing Log Outputs

Bruno allows you to customize the log outputs for easier analysis. You can choose different formats (JSON or plain text) and direct logs to specific outputs (console or file). Adjust these settings in your configuration file:

```
{
  "logging": {
    "level": "debug",
    "format": "json",
    "output": "console"
  }
}
```

With the JSON format, each log entry is structured with keys like **`timestamp`**, **`level`**, **`message`**, and **`data`**. This structure makes it easier to parse and analyze logs using command-line tools or log management systems.

All these methods and techniques gives a deeper understanding of how robust logging mechanisms can help track performance, identify bottlenecks, and streamline debugging efforts.

Summary

In short, we used Bruno's advanced features to debug and optimize our Lumina API. We traced API requests and responses in real time, capturing everything from incoming data to the final output. We set breakpoints at important points, checked variables dynamically, and logged key operations like data normalization, password hashing, and database insertions. As we analyzed the live logs, we noticed some unexpected stuff, like minor performance delays during high concurrency, which made us want to tweak our code.

We also ran through all kinds of scenarios, like normal operations, error conditions, and security checks, making sure our API responded with the right status codes and error messages. The real-time insights let us make sure that token extraction and validation in protected endpoints worked perfectly, and our logs showed us exactly how the system was performing. We also tried out some custom logging setups to help us format and direct our logs for easier analysis. Each debugging session showed us how important it is to have detailed, structured logging for both troubleshooting and performance optimization.

CHAPTER 8: AUTOMATING API TASKS

Overview

In this chapter, we're going to take a look at how to write custom automation scripts to make your API development workflow more efficient. You'll learn how to create scripts that handle testing, deployment, and data management tasks for the Lumina API. We'll start by talking about why automation is important and how it can help you reduce manual intervention in repetitive operations.

Then, you'll see some practical examples of how to write shell scripts that run tasks like testing, updating settings, and deploying your API to different environments—all with just one command. You'll also learn how to automate important data management tasks like backing up your database and seeding, so your API always has the data it needs to be ready for production. When you integrate these scripts into your continuous integration pipeline, you'll have a reliable and efficient system that quickly validates changes and deploys updates.

Automating Routine API Operations

In the previous chapters, we established a solid foundation for our Lumina API project by performing several routine operations, including:

- Setting up the project structure, installing Bruno CLI, and configuring Bru Lang to create a ready-to-use development environment.
- Building core endpoints for user registration, retrieval, updating, and deletion, while embedding business logic and handling data transformations.
- Configuring JWT authentication and OAuth 2.0 authorization to protect endpoints, as well as managing secrets to safeguard sensitive information.
- Developing automated test suites, simulating various API interactions (including high concurrency, latency, and unauthorized access), and debugging using live logs and tracing features.
- Maintaining clear documentation of API specifications, endpoints, and business rules, ensuring consistency across development and future enhancements.

These routine operations formed the backbone of our API development process. Each step, from initialization to testing, was critical for ensuring that our API met functional, performance, and security requirements.

Automating Operations with Bruno CLI

Bruno CLI has a bunch of commands that'll help you automate all those boring, repetitive tasks. It'll streamline your workflow and free up your time so you can focus on the important stuff — designing and optimizing. We're going to show you how to automate a few of the most important operations in this part.

Automating Project Initialization

When starting a new API project or setting up a new environment for Lumina API, automating the initialization process can save a significant amount of time. Bruno CLI provides commands to quickly scaffold a project with the necessary structure and configuration files.

For instance, to initialize a new project, you might run:

```
bruno init lumina-api
```

This command automatically creates the directory structure (including folders for endpoints, schemas, and documentation) and generates default configuration files.

Automating Test Suite Execution

It's always a pain to run your automated test suites manually every time you make changes. You can use the Bruno CLI to schedule and run these tests automatically. With commands like **`bruno test`**, you can trigger your entire test suite from the command line.

For example, you might integrate this command into a script:

```
#!/bin/bash
echo "Running automated test suites for Lumina API..."
bruno test
```

Saving this script as **`run_tests.sh`** and making it executable ensures that you can run your tests with a single command. Additionally, integrating this script into your continuous integration (CI) pipeline will automate the process further, running tests on every commit or pull request.

Automating Deployment Operations

Another thing that's really helpful is automating the deployment of your API after updates. Bruno CLI lets you automate deployment tasks so that your latest changes get pushed to your staging or production environments seamlessly.

For instance, you might run:

```
bruno deploy --env production
```

This command packages your API, applies the necessary configuration settings for the production environment, and deploys it automatically. You can combine this command with your CI/CD pipeline to ensure that deployments are consistent and occur without manual intervention.

Automating Configuration Updates

You can also automate managing configuration settings, like updating environment variables or secret keys. With the Bruno CLI, you can script changes to your configuration files to make sure updates are applied evenly across your environments.

For example, to update the JWT secret in your configuration, you might run a command that edits the configuration file:

```
bruno config set jwt.secret "NewSuperSecretKey"
```

This command updates the configuration, and by scripting it as part of your deployment or maintenance routine, you guarantee that your API is always running with the most secure and up-to-date settings.

Sample Program: Automating Multiple Operations

We'll make a full automation script that combines a bunch of routine operations. This script will get the project going, run tests, update settings, and deploy the API. Just save the following as **automate_lumina.sh**:

```
#!/bin/bash
# Automating Routine API Operations for Lumina API
echo "Starting automation script for Lumina API..."
# Initialize the project if not already set up
if [ ! -d "$HOME/lumina-api" ]; then
  echo "Initializing new Lumina API project..."
  bruno init lumina-api
else
  echo "Lumina API project already exists. Skipping
initialization."
fi
# Change directory to the project folder
cd "$HOME/lumina-api" || exit
# Run automated test suites to verify functionality
echo "Running automated test suites..."
bruno test
```

```
if [ $? -ne 0 ]; then
  echo "Tests failed. Aborting deployment."
  exit 1
fi
# Update configuration settings if necessary
echo "Updating configuration settings..."
bruno config set jwt.secret "NewSuperSecretKey"
bruno config set oauth.clientSecret "NewOAuthSecretKey"
# Deploy the API to the production environment
echo "Deploying Lumina API to production..."
bruno deploy --env production
if [ $? -eq 0 ]; then
  echo "Deployment completed successfully."
else
  echo "Deployment failed. Check logs for details."
fi
echo "Automation script for Lumina API finished."
```

Here,

- The script first checks if the Lumina API project directory exists. If not, it initializes a new project using **`bruno init`**.
- It then navigates to the project directory and executes the test suite with **`bruno test`**. If any tests fail, the script aborts, preventing deployment of potentially faulty code.
- The script updates critical configuration values, such as the JWT and OAuth client secrets, ensuring that these sensitive settings are current.

Finally, the script deploys the API to the production environment using **`bruno deploy --env production`**. The script checks the exit status of the deployment command and provides feedback accordingly.

Scheduling and Continuous Integration

There's more to automating routine API operations than just local scripts. Integrating these scripts into a CI/CD pipeline can improve your development workflow even more. Tools like GitHub

Actions, Jenkins, or GitLab CI can be configured to run your automation scripts on every commit or on a defined schedule. Tests are run, configurations are updated, and deployments occur seamlessly, reducing manual intervention. A simple CI configuration using GitHub Actions might include a job that executes your **automate_lumina.sh** script, ensuring that every code change is automatically validated and deployed if all tests pass.

In your daily workflow, you can run your automation scripts as part of your pre-deployment routine. This habit ensures that before any code is pushed to production, it has already passed a comprehensive battery of tests, configuration updates, and deployment checks.

Writing Custom Automation Scripts

Custom automation scripts are designed to:

- Run automated test suites with a single command, ensuring that every change in your API is validated.
- Package and deploy your API to staging or production environments effortlessly.
- Automate data management tasks like seeding databases, performing backups, and cleaning up test data.

When you write these scripts, you can turn complex operations into simple, repeatable commands that'll boost your productivity and reliability.

Script for Automated Testing

We will start by creating a custom script that runs all our automated tests. We want to ensure that before any deployment, the API passes a series of functional and security tests. So here, we will create a file named **run_tests.sh** with the following script:

```
#!/bin/bash
echo "Starting automated test suite for Lumina API..."
# Run user registration tests
echo "Running User Registration Tests..."
curl -s -X POST http://localhost:3000/users \
  -H "Content-Type: application/json" \
  -d '{
    "username": "testuser",
    "email": "testuser@gitforgits.com",
```

```
    "password": "TestPass123",
    "profile": {
      "firstName": "Test",
      "lastName": "User",
      "address": {
        "street": "100 Test St",
        "city": "Testville",
        "postalCode": "12345",
        "country": "Testland"
      },
      "contacts": [{"type": "mobile", "number": "1234567890"}]
    },
    "settings": {
      "preferences": ["news", "updates"],
      "notifications": true
    }
  }' > registration_output.txt
# Check the response status code
reg_status=$(tail -n1 registration_output.txt)
if [ "$reg_status" -eq 201 ]; then
  echo "User registration test passed with status code:
$reg_status"
else
  echo "User registration test failed with status code:
$reg_status"
  exit 1
fi
# Run user retrieval tests
echo "Running User Retrieval Tests..."
curl -s -X GET http://localhost:3000/users/1 \
```

```
  -H "Content-Type: application/json" \
  -H "Authorization: Bearer your_valid_token" >
retrieval_output.txt
retrieval_status=$(tail -n1 retrieval_output.txt)
if [ "$retrieval_status" -eq 200 ]; then
  echo "User retrieval test passed with status code:
$retrieval_status"
else
  echo "User retrieval test failed with status code:
$retrieval_status"
  exit 1
fi
echo "All tests passed successfully."
```

Now see how it works:

- The script uses **curl** commands to send HTTP requests to the Lumina API endpoints.
- The output is stored in temporary files (**registration_output.txt**, **retrieval_output.txt**), and the last line is used to extract the HTTP status code.

This script can be extended to include other test cases as required.

Script for Automated Deployment

When you use automated deployment, your API is deployed consistently and quickly whenever changes occur. You can combine deployment tasks into a single script that initializes the environment, updates configurations, and deploys the API.

Let us create a file named **deploy_api.sh** with the following script:

```
#!/bin/bash
echo "Starting Lumina API deployment..."
# Navigate to the project directory
cd "$HOME/lumina-api" || exit
# Pull the latest changes from the repository
echo "Pulling latest code changes..."
```

```
git pull origin main
# Run tests before deployment
echo "Running test suite..."
./run_tests.sh
if [ $? -ne 0 ]; then
  echo "Tests failed. Aborting deployment."
  exit 1
fi
# Update configuration settings if necessary
echo "Updating configuration settings..."
bruno config set jwt.secret "NewSuperSecretJWTKey"
bruno config set oauth.clientSecret "NewOAuthSecretKey"
# Deploy the API using Bruno CLI
echo "Deploying Lumina API..."
bruno deploy --env production
if [ $? -eq 0 ]; then
  echo "Deployment completed successfully."
else
  echo "Deployment failed. Check logs for details."
  exit 1
fi
```

And now see how it really works:

- The script navigates to the Lumina API project directory and pulls the latest code.
- It runs the test suite using the **run_tests.sh** script to ensure that the API is stable before deployment.
- Configuration settings are updated as needed using Bruno CLI commands.
- Finally, the script deploys the API to the production environment.
- The script checks the success of each command using exit statuses, ensuring a smooth deployment process.

Script for Data Management

Keeping data in order is a big part of running an API, especially when it comes to setting up the database with the first data or doing regular backups. A custom script can automate all of this, making sure everything stays in sync across different environments.

For this alos, we now create a file named **manage_data.sh** as below:

```
#!/bin/bash

echo "Starting data management tasks for Lumina API..."

# Define database backup directory and file name

BACKUP_DIR="$HOME/lumina_api_backups"

mkdir -p "$BACKUP_DIR"

BACKUP_FILE="$BACKUP_DIR/backup_$(date +%Y%m%d_%H%M%S).sql"

# Perform database backup using a hypothetical database CLI
tool

echo "Backing up the database..."

db_backup_command --host=db.gitforgits.com --user=dbuser --
password="$LUMINA_DB_PASSWORD" --database=lumina >
"$BACKUP_FILE"

if [ $? -eq 0 ]; then

  echo "Database backup completed successfully. Backup file:
$BACKUP_FILE"

else

  echo "Database backup failed. Check your database
configuration."

  exit 1

fi

# Seed the database with initial data if necessary

echo "Seeding the database with initial data..."

db_seed_command --file=seed_data.sql

if [ $? -eq 0 ]; then

  echo "Database seeding completed successfully."

else
```

```
    echo "Database seeding failed."
    exit 1
fi
```

Here, the script creates a backup directory and defines a backup file with a timestamp. It then executes a database backup command using a hypothetical database CLI tool, storing the output in the backup file.

After the backup, it runs a command to seed the database with initial data. Each command's success is verified using exit statuses, ensuring that any errors in data management are immediately caught.

By writing custom automation scripts, you save time and reduce errors, and you create a reliable, repeatable process that improves the quality of your Lumina API. You'll find these scripts become an integral part of your development workflow, ensuring that testing, deployment, and data management tasks are performed consistently and efficiently.

Exporting API Collections to Bruno

Both Postman and Insomnia provide robust environments for designing, testing, and documenting API requests. Postman, for instance, allows you to create collections of requests, organize them into folders, and manage environments and variables. Insomnia offers similar functionalities with a focus on simplicity and ease of use. Developers have long relied on these tools for their user-friendly interfaces and extensive feature sets. However, as projects evolve, teams often seek alternative solutions that offer streamlined performance and deeper integration with automated workflows. Bruno emerges as an open-source alternative that aims to consolidate API development tasks, including design, testing, and deployment, into a single, lightweight tool. The next step is to learn how to migrate the API data and configurations from Postman or Insomnia into Bruno, making it possible to leverage our existing workflows without starting from scratch.

API Collections in Postman and Insomnia

Before we begin the migration process, it's important to grasp how API collections are structured in Postman and Insomnia. A Postman collection is a group of API requests organized by folders. Each request includes details such as the URL, HTTP method, headers, body data, and test scripts. Collections are typically exported in JSON format, which preserves the structure and metadata of each request. The Insomnia exports API data in a similar JSON format, capturing the requests, environments, and configuration details that you've set up. Insomnia's export file includes details about the API endpoints and can be converted or imported into other tools.

Both tools are widely used for initial API testing and design, and migrating from them to Bruno allows you to maintain your current configurations while benefiting from Bruno's streamlined CLI-based workflow.

The migration process begins with exporting your API collections from Postman or Insomnia. In Postman, you can select the collection you want to export, choose the export option, and save the JSON file locally. In Insomnia, a similar process applies—export your workspace or collection as a JSON file. Once you have the exported JSON file, the next step is to import these configurations into Bruno.

Migrating Postman Collections

Export Collection from Postman

- Open Postman, select the collection you want to migrate, and click on the three dots next to the collection name and select **Export**.
- Next, choose the collection format and save the JSON file to your local machine, for example, **`lumina_collection.postman_collection.json`**.

Import Collection into Bruno

Bruno CLI provides an import command that can be used to migrate your Postman collection. Run the following command in your terminal:

```
bruno import --source
lumina_collection.postman_collection.json --format postman
```

This command instructs Bruno to import the collection from the specified JSON file, interpreting it as a Postman collection. The Bruno then converts the collection into its native format, mapping endpoints, request bodies, headers, and even test scripts into corresponding Bruno definitions.

Verify Imported Collection

After the import process, use Bruno's built-in tools to list the imported endpoints:

```
bruno list endpoints
```

This command displays all the endpoints imported from your Postman collection. You then verify that all the expected endpoints are present, and check if the configuration details (such as request methods, URLs, and headers) match what you had in Postman.

Following is a simple example of an endpoint definition that might be generated from your Postman collection, which you can further refine:

```
// Imported endpoint from Postman collection
```

```
endpoint /users {
  method: POST;
  request: {
    body: {
      username: string,
      email: string,
      password: string,
      profile: {
        firstName: string,
        lastName: string,
        address: {
          street: string,
          city: string,
          postalCode: string,
          country: string
        }
      }
    }
  };
  response: {
    status: 201,
    body: {
      id: number,
      username: string,
      email: string,
      createdAt: datetime
    }
  };
}
```

You can now modify this endpoint as needed to incorporate any additional logic or formatting that is unique to your Lumina API project.

Migrating Insomnia Collections

The process for migrating Insomnia collections is similar to that of Postman. You need to simply follow the below steps:

Export Collection from Insomnia

- Open Insomnia and select the workspace or collection to export.
- Go to **Application > Data > Export Data** and choose to export in JSON format.
- Save the exported file locally like, **`lumina_insomnia_export.json`**.

Import Collection into Bruno

Use Bruno's CLI to import the Insomnia collection:

```
bruno import --source lumina_insomnia_export.json --format
insomnia
```

This command tells Bruno that the source file is in Insomnia format. Bruno will parse the JSON, extract the API endpoints, and convert them into its native format.

Verify and Adjust

Again, verify the imported endpoints by listing them:

```
bruno list endpoints
```

Check that the endpoints have been imported correctly and that the request/response details match your original configurations from Insomnia. Make any necessary adjustments to environment variables, authentication, or data schemas.

Automating Migration Process

Now in this also we can make an effort to automate the migration for future projects. Here, you can simply write a custom automation script that handles the export and import steps. Below is a sample script named **`migrate_api.sh`** that automates the migration from a Postman or Insomnia collection to Bruno:

```
#!/bin/bash

# Check if a source file is provided
```

```
if [ -z "$1" ]; then
  echo "Usage: ./migrate_api.sh <collection_file.json>
[postman|insomnia]"
  exit 1
fi
COLLECTION_FILE="$1"
FORMAT="${2:-postman}"  # Default format is postman if not
specified
echo "Migrating API collection from $COLLECTION_FILE using
format $FORMAT..."
# Run the Bruno import command
bruno import --source "$COLLECTION_FILE" --format "$FORMAT"
if [ $? -eq 0 ]; then
  echo "API collection migrated successfully."
  echo "Listing imported endpoints..."
  bruno list endpoints
else
  echo "Migration failed. Please check the collection file and
format."
  exit 1
fi
```

After this, save the script as **migrate_api.sh** in your project directory and make it executable:

```
chmod +x migrate_api.sh
```

Then, run the script by specifying the collection file and its format (either **postman** or **insomnia**):

```
./migrate_api.sh lumina_collection.postman_collection.json
postman
```

This will automate the import process for you and your team to migrate collections whenever needed. Once you have reviewed and adjusted the imported collections, your Lumina API project will have a unified set of endpoints and configurations in Bruno's format. This whole integration allows you to leverage Bruno's powerful CLI and automation features to manage, test, and deploy your API efficiently. The process of migrating from tools like Postman and Insomnia not only preserves your existing workflows but also provides an opportunity to streamline and enhance your API development process with Bruno's lightweight and flexible framework.

Summary

So, we automated a bunch of key operations in our API development workflow to reduce manual effort and make things more consistent. We looked at all the routine tasks we'd previously covered, like project initialization, endpoint testing, deployment, and configuration updates, and figured out how to use the Bruno CLI to automate them. We wrote custom automation scripts using shell scripting to manage testing, deployment, and data management processes. We also dealt with moving API collections from Postman and Insomnia into Bruno. We did this by exporting our existing API configurations as JSON files and importing them into Bruno with a special command, keeping our old workflows while switching to a more integrated environment. This whole process saved us a lot of time and cut down on human error. The examples and scripts we created gave us a clear path to maintain a continuous integration pipeline, which made our API system more robust and scalable in a real-world setting.

CHAPTER 9: ADVANCED INTEGRATION AND SERVICES

Overview

In this chapter, we will explore advanced integration techniques and learn how to connect our Lumina API to various external data sources and services. You will begin by understanding the integration capabilities offered by Bruno, which allow our API to seamlessly interact with third-party platforms. We will then move into practical demonstrations, where you will export API collections from tools like Postman and Insomnia and import them into Bruno, preserving your existing workflows.

Following that, you will integrate with systems such as Jira for issue tracking, GitHub for version control, Jenkins for CI/CD automation, and AWS for cloud services, learning how to set up each connection step by step. Additionally, you will implement webhooks and event-driven actions to ensure that your API can respond dynamically to real-time data changes. By the end, you will have a robust understanding of how to extend the functionality of your Lumina API by incorporating external services, making it more scalable, interconnected, and capable of meeting diverse business needs in dynamic environments.

Connecting to External Data Sources

Bruno is designed to be highly modular, supporting integrations with various external systems through its CLI and scriptable interfaces. Its key integration capabilities include:

- Bruno can import and export data in multiple formats, making it easy to synchronize configurations, API collections, and even logs with external tools.
- Bruno supports making HTTP requests, allowing it to interact with any service that exposes REST APIs. This enables integration with tools such as Jira for issue tracking, GitHub for version control, Jenkins for continuous integration, and AWS services for cloud storage and computation.
- With its built-in scripting support, Bruno allows you to write custom scripts that automate interactions with third-party services. These scripts can be triggered via the CLI and integrated into your API workflows.
- Bruno can receive and process webhook events, facilitating real-time data exchange with external services.

With all such capabilities, you can create an API that not only handles your own data but also pulls in external data, triggers actions in other systems, and keeps everything in sync across different platforms.

Integrations with Jira, GitHub, Jenkins and AWS

We've got some handy demos below that'll walk you through integrating our Lumina API with Jira, GitHub, Jenkins, and AWS using Bruno's features.

Integrating with Jira

Jira is commonly used for issue tracking and project management. With Bruno, you can automate the process of creating issues in Jira when your API encounters specific errors or performance issues.

So here, first you obtain your Jira API credentials (API token, username, and Jira domain) and store them securely in environment variables:

```
export JIRA_DOMAIN="your-jira-domain.atlassian.net"
export JIRA_USERNAME="your_email@gitforgits.com"
export JIRA_API_TOKEN="your_jira_api_token"
```

next, create a script named **create_jira_issue.bru** that sends a POST request to Jira's issue creation endpoint:

```
// create_jira_issue.bru
// This script creates a new Jira issue when an API error
occurs.
function createJiraIssue(summary, description) {
  let jiraUrl = "https://" + env.JIRA_DOMAIN +
"/rest/api/3/issue";
  let payload = {
    "fields": {
      "project": {
        "key": "LUM"  // Replace with your Jira project key
      },
      "summary": summary,
      "description": description,
      "issuetype": {
        "name": "Bug"
      }
    }
  };
  // Basic authentication header creation
```

```
  let authString = env.JIRA_USERNAME + ":" +
env.JIRA_API_TOKEN;
  let authHeader = "Basic " +
security.base64Encode(authString);
  // Execute the HTTP POST request
  let response = http.post(jiraUrl, {
    headers: {
      "Content-Type": "application/json",
      "Authorization": authHeader
    },
    body: JSON.stringify(payload)
  });
  if (response.status == 201) {
    bruno.debug.log("Jira issue created successfully:",
response.body);
  } else {
    bruno.debug.log("Failed to create Jira issue. Status:",
response.status, "Response:", response.body);
  }
}
// Example usage: create a Jira issue with error details
createJiraIssue("Lumina API Error", "An error occurred during
API processing. Check logs for details.");
```

This script defines a function to create a Jira issue by constructing the appropriate payload and sending a POST request with the necessary authentication. You can trigger this script from your error-handling logic in your API when critical issues are detected.

Integrating with GitHub

The GitHub integration can help you automate tasks like creating issues from error logs or updating repository statuses after deployments. To do this, first store your GitHub access token and repository details as environment variables:

```
export GITHUB_REPO="username/lumina-api"
```

```
export GITHUB_TOKEN="your_github_access_token"
```

Next, create a script named **create_github_issue.bru**:

```
// create_github_issue.bru
// This script creates a GitHub issue to log critical API
errors.
function createGitHubIssue(title, body) {
  let githubUrl = "https://api.github.com/repos/" +
env.GITHUB_REPO + "/issues";
  let payload = {
    "title": title,
    "body": body
  };
  // Set up the Authorization header with the GitHub token
  let authHeader = "token " + env.GITHUB_TOKEN;
  let response = http.post(githubUrl, {
    headers: {
      "Content-Type": "application/json",
      "Authorization": authHeader
    },
    body: JSON.stringify(payload)
  });
  if (response.status == 201) {
    bruno.debug.log("GitHub issue created successfully:",
response.body);
  } else {
    bruno.debug.log("Failed to create GitHub issue. Status:",
response.status, "Response:", response.body);
  }
}
```

```
// Example usage: create a GitHub issue for a detected error
createGitHubIssue("Lumina API Critical Error", "A critical error occurred in the API. Immediate investigation required.");
```

This script interacts with GitHub's API to create an issue in the specified repository, providing a seamless way to track issues detected during API operations.

Integrating with Jenkins

Coming to Jenkins, this can be integrated to trigger CI/CD pipelines or run additional tests when certain API events occur. Similar to GitHub and Jira, first you need to store your Jenkins server URL, job name, and API token as environment variables:

```
export JENKINS_URL="https://jenkins.yourdomain.com"
export JENKINS_JOB="Lumina_API_Build"
export JENKINS_TOKEN="your_jenkins_api_token"
```

Next, create a script named **trigger_jenkins_job.bru**:

```
// trigger_jenkins_job.bru
// This script triggers a Jenkins job for Lumina API build or tests.
function triggerJenkinsJob() {
  let jenkinsUrl = env.JENKINS_URL + "/job/" + env.JENKINS_JOB + "/build?token=" + env.JENKINS_TOKEN;
  let response = http.post(jenkinsUrl, {
    headers: { "Content-Type": "application/json" }
  });
  if (response.status == 201 || response.status == 200) {
    bruno.debug.log("Jenkins job triggered successfully:", response.body);
  } else {
    bruno.debug.log("Failed to trigger Jenkins job. Status:", response.status, "Response:", response.body);
  }
```

```
}
// Example usage: trigger Jenkins job on deployment
triggerJenkinsJob();
```

This script sends a POST request to your Jenkins server to trigger a specific job, automating your build and deployment processes whenever needed.

Integrating with AWS

When you integrate with AWS, you can use a bunch of different services like S3 for storage, EC2 for hosting, or Lambda for serverless functions. For this demo, we're going to focus on connecting to AWS S3 to upload logs or backup data.

Here also, first store your AWS credentials and bucket name as environment variables:

```
export AWS_ACCESS_KEY_ID="your_aws_access_key_id"
export AWS_SECRET_ACCESS_KEY="your_aws_secret_access_key"
export AWS_REGION="your_aws_region"
export AWS_S3_BUCKET="your_s3_bucket_name"
```

Then as usual, write a script named **`upload_to_s3.bru`**:

```
// upload_to_s3.bru
// This script uploads a file to an AWS S3 bucket.
function uploadToS3(filePath) {
  let s3Url = "https://" + env.AWS_S3_BUCKET + ".s3." +
env.AWS_REGION + ".amazonaws.com/" + filePath;


  // Prepare headers for AWS Signature (simplified; real
implementation requires signature generation)
  let headers = {
    "Content-Type": "application/octet-stream",
    "x-amz-acl": "private",
    // The following headers should be generated via AWS
Signature Version 4
```

```
    "Authorization": "AWS4-HMAC-SHA256 Credential=" +
env.AWS_ACCESS_KEY_ID + "/...signature details..."
  };
  // Read file content (assuming a function exists to read
file content)
  let fileContent = file.read(filePath);
  let response = http.put(s3Url, {
    headers: headers,
    body: fileContent
  });
  if (response.status == 200) {
    bruno.debug.log("File uploaded successfully to S3:",
filePath);
  } else {
    bruno.debug.log("Failed to upload file to S3. Status:",
response.status, "Response:", response.body);
  }
}
// Example usage: upload a backup file to S3
uploadToS3("backup_20230501.sql");
```

This script uploads file to AWS S3. In a production scenario, you would generate proper AWS signatures to authenticate the request.

Each integration scenario showcased above teaches you to bridge your API with external platforms helping your various operations such as issue tracking, version control, CI/CD triggering, and cloud storage. These integrations not only extend the functionality of your API but also facilitate smoother collaboration and efficient workflow management.

Implementing Webhooks and Event-Driven Actions

Webhooks are basically custom HTTP callbacks that get triggered by certain events like user registrations, updates to resources, or error conditions. When something like this happens, our

API can send an HTTP POST request to a URL we've already set up with the relevant info. This lets external systems or services know right away about the event.

Event-driven actions, on the other hand, are internal processes that get started in response to events. These actions might include sending notifications, updating logs, triggering additional API calls, or even invoking other microservices. Since we designed our API with event-driven principles, our system can adapt and react promptly to changes, leading to more resilient and interactive applications.

Configuring Webhooks

Define Webhook Endpoints

The first step is to define webhook endpoints in our API where external systems can send event notifications. For example, you might create a webhook endpoint that listens for events such as user registration or updates.

Given below is a sample endpoint definition:

```
// Webhook Endpoint to Receive Notifications
endpoint /webhooks/notifications {
  method: POST;
  request: {
    body: {
      eventType: string,        // e.g., "USER_CREATED",
"USER_UPDATED"
      payload: object           // Contains event-specific data
    }
  };
  logic: {
    // Log the received webhook event for auditing
    bruno.debug.log("Received Webhook Event:", request.body);
    // Process the event based on its type
    if (request.body.eventType == "USER_CREATED") {
      // Perform actions such as updating a dashboard or
triggering further processing
      bruno.debug.log("Processing USER_CREATED event.");
```

```
        // Custom logic to handle user creation events
    } else if (request.body.eventType == "USER_UPDATED") {
        bruno.debug.log("Processing USER_UPDATED event.");
        // Custom logic to handle user updates
    } else {
        bruno.debug.log("Received unknown event type:",
request.body.eventType);
    }
    return response(200, {
        message: "Webhook event processed successfully."
    });
  };
  error: {
    400: {
        error: "InvalidInput",
        message: "Webhook payload is missing required fields."
    }
  }
}
```

In this endpoint, when a webhook notification is received, it logs the event, determines the event type, and processes it accordingly. This basic setup ensures that our API is ready to accept and respond to incoming webhook events.

Register Webhook URLs

Once the webhook endpoint is defined, the next step is to register the URL with the external service that will be sending notifications. For instance, if integrating with a service like GitHub, you can configure the repository settings to send webhook notifications to **`https://your-api-domain/webhooks/notifications`**. This step is done through the external service's interface rather than directly in Bruno, but it is crucial to ensure that the endpoint is reachable and properly secured.

Triggering Event-Driven Actions

Define Event Sources and Triggers

Event-driven actions within our API are triggered by internal events. For example, when a new user is created, we might want to automatically send a welcome email or update a user analytics dashboard. In our API logic, we can incorporate event triggers to call specific functions or even external APIs.

So let us think of a scenario where, after successful user registration, we want to trigger an internal event that sends a welcome email. For this, we can define an event function as shown below:

```
// Function to trigger a welcome email event
function triggerWelcomeEmail(user) {
  // Log the action for auditing purposes
  bruno.debug.log("Triggering welcome email for user:",
user.email);

  // Simulate sending an email by making a POST request to an
email service
  let emailServiceUrl = "https://email-
service.gitforgits.com/send";
  let emailPayload = {
    to: user.email,
    subject: "Welcome to Lumina API!",
    body: "Dear " + user.profile.firstName + ", welcome to our
platform. We are excited to have you on board."
  };

  let emailResponse = http.post(emailServiceUrl, {
    headers: { "Content-Type": "application/json" },
    body: JSON.stringify(emailPayload)
  });

  // Log the response from the email service
  bruno.debug.log("Email service response:", emailResponse);
```

```
  return emailResponse;
}
```

Integrate Event Triggers into Endpoint Logic

Just add the above event trigger to your user registration endpoint so that when a new user is created, the welcome email event is automatically triggered.

```
endpoint /users {
  method: POST;
  request: {
    body: {
      username: string,
      email: string,
      password: string,
      profile: {
        firstName: string,
        lastName: string,
        address: {
          street: string,
          city: string,
          postalCode: string,
          country: string
        },
        contacts: [
          {
            type: string,
            number: string
          }
        ],
```

```
        socialMedia?: {
          twitter: string?,
          facebook: string?,
          instagram: string?
        }
      },
      settings: {
        preferences: [string],
        notifications: boolean
      }
    }
  };
  logic: {
    // Log incoming request
    bruno.debug.log("Processing user registration:",
request.body);

    // Normalize and process data
    request.body.email = request.body.email.toLowerCase();
    request.body.password =
security.hash(request.body.password);
    request.body.createdAt = datetime.now();

    // Insert user into the database
    let newUser = db.insert("users", request.body);
    bruno.debug.log("New user inserted:", newUser);

    // Trigger a welcome email event after successful
registration
    let emailResult = triggerWelcomeEmail(newUser);
```

```
    bruno.debug.log("Welcome email event triggered:",
emailResult);

    // Optionally, trigger additional event-driven actions
(e.g., update analytics)
    // ...

    return response(201, {
      id: newUser.id,
      username: newUser.username,
      email: newUser.email,
      profile: newUser.profile,
      settings: newUser.settings,
      createdAt: newUser.createdAt
    });
  };
  error: {
    400: {
      error: "InvalidInput",
      message: "Required fields are missing or invalid."
    }
  }
}
```

Here, after the new user is inserted into the database, the **`triggerWelcomeEmail`** function is called. The API logs both the action and the result of the email service call. This demonstrates a simple event-driven action where an internal event (user creation) automatically triggers an external action (sending an email).

Simulating External Event Responses

To further explore event-driven actions, you can simulate an external event, such as an update notification from another system, that triggers a corresponding action in your API. For example, if an external system sends a webhook notifying you of an update to a user's profile, your webhook endpoint can capture that event and initiate a data synchronization process.

```
// Webhook Endpoint to Handle Profile Update Notifications
endpoint /webhooks/profile-update {
  method: POST;
  request: {
    body: {
      eventType: string,   // Should be "PROFILE_UPDATED"
      payload: {
        userId: number,
        updatedFields: object  // Contains fields that were
updated
      }
    }
  };
  logic: {
    bruno.debug.log("Received profile update webhook:",
request.body);

    if (request.body.eventType == "PROFILE_UPDATED") {
      // Fetch the current user data
      let user = db.find("users", { id:
request.body.payload.userId });
      if (!user) {
        return error(404, {
          error: "NotFound",
          message: "User not found for the provided ID."
        });
      }
```

```
        // Update the user profile based on the webhook payload
        let updatedUser = db.update("users", { id: user.id },
request.body.payload.updatedFields);
        bruno.debug.log("User profile updated via webhook:",
updatedUser);

        // Optionally, trigger further actions, e.g., send
notification to the user
        // triggerProfileUpdateNotification(updatedUser);

        return response(200, {
          message: "User profile updated successfully via
webhook."
        });
      } else {
        return error(400, {
          error: "InvalidEvent",
          message: "Unsupported event type received."
        });
      }
    };
    error: {
      400: {
        error: "InvalidInput",
        message: "The webhook payload is missing required
fields."
      }
    }
}
```

In the above script, the webhook endpoint listens for profile update notifications. When a valid event is received, it logs the payload, retrieves the current user data, and updates the profile accordingly. You can also extend this to trigger additional notifications or synchronizations.

Testing Webhook and Event-Driven Actions

If you want to make sure everything works right, you should use the tools you have to simulate webhook events and see the actions that happen because of them. For example, simply use **`curl`** to send a test payload to the **`/webhooks/profile-update`** endpoint:

```
curl -X POST http://localhost:3000/webhooks/profile-update \
  -H "Content-Type: application/json" \
  -d '{
    "eventType": "PROFILE_UPDATED",
    "payload": {
      "userId": 1,
      "updatedFields": {
        "profile": {
          "firstName": "UpdatedFirstName",
          "lastName": "UpdatedLastName"
        }
      }
    }
  }'
```

Just check the console logs to confirm that the webhook is received, processed, and that the user profile is updated as expected. After a user registration, make sure that the welcome email event is triggered by checking the logs. You'll also want to ensure that the call to the external email service (simulated in our script) is logged and that the response from that service is captured.

Testing and Validating Third-Party Integrations

Third-party integration testing ensures that external services are correctly connected, authenticated, and that data flows seamlessly between our API and these services. So now, we will go through practical tests for each integration and demonstrate how to validate that every piece of the external connection is functioning properly.

Testing Jira Integration

To begin, simply write a shell script named **test_jira_issue.sh**:

```
#!/bin/bash
# Define variables for Jira
JIRA_DOMAIN="your-jira-domain.atlassian.net"
JIRA_USERNAME="your_email@gitforgits.com"
JIRA_API_TOKEN="your_jira_api_token"
PROJECT_KEY="LUM"  # Your Jira project key
# Prepare the payload
payload=$(cat <<EOF
{
  "fields": {
    "project": {
      "key": "${PROJECT_KEY}"
    },
    "summary": "Test Issue from Lumina API",
    "description": "This is a test issue created by the Lumina API integration.",
    "issuetype": {
      "name": "Bug"
    }
  }
}
EOF
)
# Construct the basic auth header
auth=$(echo -n "${JIRA_USERNAME}:${JIRA_API_TOKEN}" | base64)
# Send the POST request to Jira API
```

```
response=$(curl -s -w "\n%{http_code}" -X POST
"https://${JIRA_DOMAIN}/rest/api/3/issue" \
  -H "Content-Type: application/json" \
  -H "Authorization: Basic ${auth}" \
  -d "${payload}")
# Split the response into body and status code
body=$(echo "$response" | sed '$d')
status=$(echo "$response" | tail -n1)
if [ "$status" -eq 201 ]; then
  echo "Jira integration test passed. Issue created
successfully."
else
  echo "Jira integration test failed. Status code: $status"
  echo "Response body: $body"
fi
```

Make the script executable and run it:

```
chmod +x test_jira_issue.sh
./test_jira_issue.sh
```

If the test passes, you should see confirmation that the issue was created. If not, you need to check the response body for error details and adjust your integration accordingly.

Testing GitHub Integration

Similar to Jira, the goal here is to verify that our API can send correctly formatted requests and receive the proper responses. Here also, simply write a shell script named **test_github_issue.sh**:

```
#!/bin/bash
# Define GitHub variables
GITHUB_REPO="username/lumina-api"
GITHUB_TOKEN="your_github_access_token"
# Prepare the payload
```

```
payload=$(cat <<EOF
{
  "title": "Test Issue from Lumina API",
  "body": "This is a test issue generated to validate GitHub
integration."
}
EOF
)
# GitHub API endpoint for creating issues
api_url="https://api.github.com/repos/${GITHUB_REPO}/issues"
# Send POST request to create an issue
response=$(curl -s -w "\n%{http_code}" -X POST "$api_url" \
  -H "Content-Type: application/json" \
  -H "Authorization: token ${GITHUB_TOKEN}" \
  -d "${payload}")
body=$(echo "$response" | sed '$d')
status=$(echo "$response" | tail -n1)
if [ "$status" -eq 201 ]; then
  echo "GitHub integration test passed. Issue created
successfully."
else
  echo "GitHub integration test failed. Status code: $status"
  echo "Response body: $body"
fi
```

Make the script executable and run:

```
chmod +x test_github_issue.sh
./test_github_issue.sh
```

You need to review the output to ensure that an issue was created in your specified repository. You may also make use of the GitHub web interface to confirm the issue details.

Testing Jenkins Integration

Testing Jenkins integration involves triggering a Jenkins job from our API. We can simulate this by invoking our Jenkins endpoint and verifying that the job is queued.

So here, let us create a script named **test_jenkins_job.sh**:

```
#!/bin/bash
# Define Jenkins variables
JENKINS_URL="https://jenkins.yourdomain.com"
JENKINS_JOB="Lumina_API_Build"
JENKINS_TOKEN="your_jenkins_api_token"
# Construct the Jenkins job URL
jenkins_api="${JENKINS_URL}/job/${JENKINS_JOB}/build?token=${J
ENKINS_TOKEN}"
# Send the POST request to trigger the Jenkins job
response=$(curl -s -w "\n%{http_code}" -X POST "$jenkins_api"
\
  -H "Content-Type: application/json")
status=$(echo "$response" | tail -n1)
if [ "$status" -eq 201 ] || [ "$status" -eq 200 ]; then
  echo "Jenkins integration test passed. Job triggered
successfully."
else
  echo "Jenkins integration test failed. Status code: $status"
  echo "Response: $response"
fi
```

Make it executable and run:

```
chmod +x test_jenkins_job.sh
./test_jenkins_job.sh
```

You need to just check your Jenkins dashboard to see if the job was triggered. If it failed, you then need to verify your API token and URL configurations.

Testing AWS Integration

For AWS integration, we need to simulate uploading a file to an S3 bucket. This will validate that our API can interact with AWS services using appropriate credentials and configurations.

So, let us create a script named **test_s3_upload.sh**:

```
#!/bin/bash
# Define AWS variables
AWS_S3_BUCKET="your_s3_bucket_name"
AWS_REGION="your_aws_region"
FILE_PATH="test_upload.txt"
# Create a sample file to upload
echo "This is a test file for AWS S3 upload." > $FILE_PATH
# Construct the S3 URL (simplified; real implementations
require signing)
s3_url="https://${AWS_S3_BUCKET}.s3.${AWS_REGION}.amazonaws.co
m/${FILE_PATH}"
# For this simulation, we assume that Bruno's http.put
function or curl will be used
response=$(curl -s -w "\n%{http_code}" -X PUT "$s3_url" \
  -H "Content-Type: text/plain" \
  --data-binary @"$FILE_PATH")
body=$(echo "$response" | sed '$d')
status=$(echo "$response" | tail -n1)
if [ "$status" -eq 200 ]; then
  echo "AWS S3 integration test passed. File uploaded
successfully."
else
  echo "AWS S3 integration test failed. Status code: $status"
  echo "Response body: $body"
fi
```

Make the script executable:

```
chmod +x test_s3_upload.sh
./test_s3_upload.sh
```

Look over the output and check your S3 bucket to confirm the file was uploaded.

Validating Webhooks and Event-Driven Actions

To ensure that our webhooks and event-driven actions are functioning correctly, we need to simulate events and observe the responses. To do this, let us assume that we have a webhook endpoint **/webhooks/profile-update** as defined earlier.

After this, create a script named **test_webhook.sh**:

```
#!/bin/bash
WEBHOOK_URL="http://localhost:3000/webhooks/profile-update"
payload=$(cat <<EOF
{
  "eventType": "PROFILE_UPDATED",
  "payload": {
    "userId": 1,
    "updatedFields": {
      "profile": {
        "firstName": "NewFirstName",
        "lastName": "NewLastName"
      }
    }
  }
}
EOF
)
response=$(curl -s -w "\n%{http_code}" -X POST "$WEBHOOK_URL"
\
  -H "Content-Type: application/json" \
  -d "$payload")
```

```
body=$(echo "$response" | sed '$d')
status=$(echo "$response" | tail -n1)
if [ "$status" -eq 200 ]; then
  echo "Webhook integration test passed. Status code: $status"
  echo "Response: $body"
else
  echo "Webhook integration test failed. Status code: $status"
  echo "Response: $body"
fi
chmod +x test_webhook.sh
./test_webhook.sh
```

After running this, check the logs from Lumina API to verify that the webhook event was received, processed, and the correct actions were triggered (e.g., updating the user profile).

Automated Testing of Third-Party Integrations

We can consolidate all these above tests into a master script that runs all integration tests sequentially to simplify repeated validation. To do this, just create a master script named **run_integration_tests.sh**:

```
#!/bin/bash
echo "Starting integration tests for Lumina API..."
echo "Testing Jira integration..."
./test_jira_issue.sh
echo "Testing GitHub integration..."
./test_github_issue.sh
echo "Testing Jenkins integration..."
./test_jenkins_job.sh
echo "Testing AWS S3 integration..."
./test_s3_upload.sh
echo "Testing webhook integration..."
./test_webhook.sh
```

```
echo "Integration tests completed."
chmod +x run_integration_tests.sh
./run_integration_tests.sh
```

Run the script, and you will witness that the master script will sequentially execute each integration test and print the results. This ensures that all third-party integrations and webhook/event-driven actions are validated in one comprehensive run.

Summary

Finally, in this last chapter, we took our Lumina API to the next level by adding advanced third-party services and setting up real-time event responses. We checked out how Bruno could link up with other platforms like Jira, GitHub, Jenkins, and AWS, and how to bring our API collections from tools like Postman and Insomnia into Bruno. This let us keep our workflows while switching to a more streamlined setup.

We also got to know about webhooks, which let our API send and receive notifications, allowing for dynamic interactions with external systems. We practiced writing scripts that triggered actions based on specific events, like sending welcome emails after user registration and updating profiles when a webhook signaled a change. The hands-on examples showed the practical use of authentication, error handling, and data validation techniques in the context of integrations. Basically, we made sure our API could do its main job and also connect with other tools, which sets the stage for a strong system that can grow and adapt to changing business needs.

Index

W

Epilogue

I'm proud of our progress together. We've learned a lot using Bruno to manage the entire API lifecycle. From the beginning days of designing clear API blueprints to the final stages of automated testing and secure deployment, every lesson in this book has been a stepping stone to mastering a streamlined, efficient workflow. I saw for myself how Bruno's command-line strength and easy-to-use scripting tools took something that was once a huge challenge and turned it into something that was easy and even fun.

With Bruno, I learned to set up a modern development environment that gets rid of repetitive manual tasks, so I can focus on creative problem-solving. The hands-on exercises helped me add business logic directly to my endpoints and make sure I had solid error handling in place. This showed me I can trust the system to work like a charm, even when things get tough. I learned so much, like how to do automated testing and debugging. That makes the API more reliable and lets me improve it right away. I also learned how to use third-party services like Jira, GitHub, Jenkins, and AWS to expand the functionality of my API beyond its initial design. Setting up webhooks and event-driven actions showed me that real-time responsiveness is totally doable. Now, with Bruno, I've got full confidence that every part of API management, from design and coding to security and deployment, can be handled from start to finish in one environment.

All the lessons I learned on this project have empowered me to manage APIs independently and effectively. I can now design, build, test, deploy, and monitor my API with a single, cohesive tool that integrates all these essential operations.

As I move forward, I am excited to apply these skills in real-world scenarios and witness firsthand the impact of a well-managed, resilient API.

--Lyria Tharax

Thank You

www.ingramcontent.com/pod-product-compliance
Lightning Source LLC
Chambersburg PA
CBHW080212170726
48282CB00030B/1082
9788198431639